Robert James Merrell. 21/-

SOME
SHAKESPEAREAN THEMES

SOME
SHAKESPEAREAN
THEMES

by
L. C. KNIGHTS
*Winterstoke Professor of English in
the University of Bristol*

1964
CHATTO & WINDUS
LONDON

PUBLISHED BY
CHATTO AND WINDUS LTD
42 WILLIAM IV STREET
LONDON WC2

*

CLARKE, IRWIN AND CO. LTD
TORONTO

FIRST PUBLISHED 1959
REPRINTED 1960 AND 1964

PRINTED IN GREAT BRITAIN BY
T. AND A. CONSTABLE LTD
HOPETOUN STREET EDINBURGH

CONTENTS

To
R. H. TAWNEY
with gratitude and admiration

'We do not understand Shakespeare from a single reading, and certainly not from a single play. There is a relation between the various plays of Shakespeare, taken in order; and it is a work of years to venture even one individual interpretation of the pattern in Shakespeare's carpet.'

T. S. ELIOT

Foreword

THIS book is based on the belief that Shakespeare's plays form a coherent whole, that they stem from and express a developing 'attitude to life'—which does not mean that individually they were not also a response to outside demands, such as those of a particular audience. Shakespeare however could have satisfied his audience in very different ways from those that he did in fact choose to follow, so it does not seem rash to assume that he wrote about what interested him. I have further assumed that his interests were not those of the detached spectator intent solely on 'understanding' different types of human nature, and that in any play he chose to present one kind of person, one kind of plot, rather than another because in that way he could best express his sense of life's meanings. As M. Fluchère has said,

> From play to play . . . the themes become more and more closely associated with the characters and the situations. Each drama, each comedy raises one or more problems—not only those of the particular play but those resulting from an ever more serious application of thought, seconded by emotion, to the infinitely various aspects of the human condition . . . [Shakespeare] seeks to attain the deepest and most authentic human reality.[1]

I have tried to suggest some of the lines of thought that lead into the great tragedies, and to see the tragedies themselves as in some sense the resolution of pressures and perplexities to be found in the plays that precede them. The procedure is almost inevitably highly selective;

9

most of the plays before the tragedies receive scant attention, and the latest plays none at all; but to become aware of connexions even within a limited area is not only to get fresh insight into the development of Shakespeare's thought as a whole, it is to deepen our understanding of the individual plays. The charge that my selection of material is in the interests of a case to be made can only be met by the book itself, not by the partial pleadings of its author.

The book, then, is an attempt to follow certain lines of thought in some of Shakespeare's major plays; but even this description is one that immediately requires quali-fication. Shakespeare was 'the greatest of all Tudor thinkers' [2] but clearly he was not someone who 'thought out' problems intellectually before finding a dramatic form in which to embody them; he was an artist working under the conditions of his rôle as a provider of stage plays, and to understand the nature of his thinking it is necessary to understand the nature of his art, which fuses 'thought' within a wider imaginative vision. In Chapter One I glance at some significant shifts of direction in Shakespeare criticism of the last thirty years, in order to make plain the assumptions on which I have proceeded in trying to elicit some of the main lines of Shakespeare's imaginative interpretation of life—his 'thought', if we choose to call it such, though we can hardly do so without asking ourselves some fundamental questions about the relation of thought to other modes of apprehension and awareness in any creative encounter with reality.

Anyone who takes his place in the multitude of writers about Shakespeare, 'whereof the whole multitude of writers most reasonably complains', is of course uncom-fortably aware that there are already more books about Shakespeare than we can read, that is, if we want to read Shakespeare or anything else. But it is worth recalling the function that books such as this are meant to serve. We reach our understanding of literature, assimilate it, in some sense make it our own, not only when we are in direct contact with 'the words on the page'. New insights can take place when, apparently otherwise engaged, we recall what we have read, when we listen—or half-listen—to a lecture, or in talk with a friend. A book of criticism is an offer of conversation. Taken as such, taken, above all, as incitement to re-read and re-think, it has its place in the endless complex process through which literature is kept alive, and the multiplication of criticism (however much, at times, we may deplore it) is as inevitable as talk about the books we like. It is of course to be hoped that the critic has a point of view that makes conversation with him worth while. But a work of criticism with which we find conversation impossible can easily be shut up, and a book cannot pursue us down the length of the Sacred Way.

★　　★　　★

It remains to add that my own 'conversation' with Shakespeare critics of this century—from Bradley, through G. Wilson Knight, to more recent writers such as Derek Traversi, Henri Fluchère, J. F. Danby and Arthur Sewell —that this conversation has now gone on for so long that I find it impossible to list my more general indebtedness, either for suggestions that have been followed up or for challenges to disagreement. Particular obligations are, I trust, recorded. Since parts of the book were written for different purposes over a considerable period, I have not found it possible to avoid a certain amount of overlapping, perhaps even of repetition, at places where I have tried to knit together the general argument. I am grateful for permission to make use of material that originally appeared in *Scrutiny*, *The Sewanee Review*, and the *Pelican Guide to English Literature, 2, The Age of Shakespeare*.

References, notes and specific acknowledgements are reserved for the end of the book. If the text seems to me to give adequate reference to works from which I have quoted I have not given more detailed information in the notes. Quotations from Shakespeare are usually from the current Arden edition of the separate plays. If standard editions of Shakespeare's contemporaries from whom I have quoted use the original spelling I have retained this at the cost of consistency.

L. C. K.

On Some Contemporary Trends in Shakespeare Criticism and Other Preliminary Considerations

I

IT is an obvious fact that the appreciation of Shakespeare, the kind of thing men have got from Shakespeare, has varied enormously at different periods. Of course no single mode of appreciation was ever completely dominant; and between critics sharing a roughly similar manner of approach there have been great differences of critical intelligence, of degree of exposure to the plays, so that the good critic of any one phase remains valuable long after that phase has passed. But from time to time major shifts of attention occur, and not the least significant and fruitful of these is the one that has taken place in our own time, and that scholars and critics of very different kinds have helped to bring about. Conceptions of the nature and function of poetic drama have been radically revised; the essential structure of the plays has been sought in the poetry rather than in the more easily extractable elements of 'plot' and 'character'; and our whole conception of Shakespeare's relation to his work, of the kind of thing he was trying to do as an artist whilst simultaneously satisfying the demands of the Elizabethan theatre—this conception has undergone a revolutionary change. The 'new' Shakespeare, I should say, is much less impersonal than the old. Whereas in the older view Shakespeare was the god-like creator of a peopled world, projecting—it is true—his own spirit into the inhabitants, but remaining essentially the analyst of 'their' passions,

13

he is now felt as much more immediately engaged in the action he puts before us[1].

Now I think that these newer trends point to something that is genuinely *there* in Shakespeare's plays, that had been obscured by prepossessions deriving from earlier phases of Shakespeare criticism, and that is of great importance. I also think that it would be a great misfortune if the newer approach—which, in its turn, has recently been challenged[2]—were to develop into a new orthodoxy offering nothing better than a new formula to be applied more or less mechanically: far better some personal appreciation of Shakespeare's portrayal of 'character' or of 'the passions' than that! So there are two reasons why a book that is supposed to be about some Shakespearean themes should start by bringing to light the assumptions that it makes about the poetry. The first we have just glanced at: one wants to encourage thought about the way the plays work, not to promote an orthodoxy. The other is more fundamental. If, in recent Shakespeare criticism, the verse has moved well into the centre of the picture, this is because linguistic vitality is now felt as the chief clue to the urgent personal themes that not only shape the poetic-dramatic structure of each play but form the figure in the carpet of the canon as a whole. It seems as well, therefore, to present one's critical credentials and to explain something of the discipline that is involved in disengaging for attention themes that are not always on the surface.

Some years ago Professor Oscar James Campbell, in an essay called, 'Shakespeare and the "New" Critics'[3], discussed what seemed to him the ill-founded assumption that intensive analysis of imagery might lead to the discovery of a play's 'inner imaginative structure'. I am not concerned here with the justice or otherwise of his observations on particular pieces of work by two critics—

they were Cleanth Brooks and D. A. Traversi—but only with the grounds of his disagreement from them. These are, I think, fairly indicated by the following:

> The principal reason for the failure of these inter-preters . . . [is that] they approach each play of Shakespeare under a compulsion to find in his poetry those characteristics which T. S. Eliot and his followers have decided must be present in all pure poetry. They assume therefore that Shakespeare, like Donne, con-structed an integrated system of connotation based on the iteration of certain words, to which the poet had given an arbitrary symbolical value. And they make the further assumption that in this system of sequence and repetition of images all the poetry of the play is fused into one intense impression.
>
> But Shakespeare seems never to have manipulated his imagery in this consciously scheming fashion. His poetry rather gives the effect of a spontaneous eruption from that secret region of the mind where the imagin-ative impulse is generated. His imagination usually finds release, not in an integrated structure of figures, but rather in a medley of metaphors, each one relevant only to some specific emotional situation . . .
>
> The truth is [Professor Campbell concludes] that Shakespeare employed his images for two purposes, both dramatic. He made his figurative language intensify an auditor's response to particular situations and also used it to create and individualize his characters.

That, apart from a suggestion that imagery helps to create 'mood', is all that is allowed to the imagery of a Shakespeare play: to attempt to find more in it is to stray into 'the wasteland of paradox, ambiguity, and esoteric symbolism.'

If we feel that observations such as these are not critically useful, that they are blurred and out of focus,

15

how can we justify alternative critical principles that give due recognition to precisely those elements that Professor Campbell seems bent on excluding?[4]

It is the function of imagery that Professor Campbell is mainly concerned with. Let us take one of his own examples. He refers us to Lady Macbeth's words to her husband,—

> I have given suck, and know
> How tender 'tis to love the babe that milks me:
> I would, while it was smiling in my face,
> Have pluck'd my nipple from his boneless gums,
> And dash'd the brains out, had I so sworn as you
> Have done to this.

This, we are told, has a 'stark simplicity. . . . What she says to her husband is this: Rather than be such an irresolute coward as you now are, I had rather be guilty of the most fiendishly unnatural deed of which a mother is capable.' Well, she does say that. But is that all she says? We can, at all events, hardly fail to be impressed by the violence of the image, and we may legitimately regard the violence of tone as a part of the meaning of what Lady Macbeth says. The play, after all, is about a succession of violent acts—culminating in the murder of Macduff's babes—which are continually reflected in violent imagery, 'to bathe in reeking wounds', 'even till destruction sicken', and so on. But the particular choice of image in Lady Macbeth's speech surely does more than this. It is not only an image of violence, but of unnatural violence, and thus links with the insistence on 'unnatural deeds' so pervasive throughout the play that illustration is unnecessary. And the violence expressed by Lady Macbeth is directed not only towards others but towards herself. She is attempting, as she bids her husband a moment later, to 'screw her courage to the sticking-place'; and this—like Macbeth's

16

I am settled, and *bend up*
Each corporal agent to this terrible feat—

evokes an unnatural tension of the will ('I have no spur
To prick the sides of my intent . . .') which is certainly
part of the play's dramatic substance, whatever our views
about the nature of poetic drama. The lines, in short,
reverberate, and there is a process of what I. A. Richards
calls interinanimation between the image on which we
are focusing and some scores of others throughout the
play. And this, surely, is one of the ways in which the
poetic mind works when fully engaged at the deepest
levels.

We may push our enquiry a little further. When does
imagery exercise this mutually attractive power, which
issues in something not merely relevant to character or
the immediate situation? When we enlist in our interpretation of a Shakespearean tragedy a pattern of
imagery, what guarantee have we that we are not behav-
ing in an arbitrary fashion? To this last question a short
answer, and in the end the only one, is that our only
safeguard is our own ability to read poetry: lacking that
we can play any wilful tricks we like, and foist on Shakespeare, or any other dramatist, such schematic interpretations as our ingenuity can construct. But rational
argument consists in expanding short answers into longer
ones, and I return to my question.

In the fifth act of *King John*, when the King is dying and
the revolted English lords are about to return to their
allegiance, these lines occur:

But even this night, whose black contagious breath
Already smokes about the burning crest
Of the old, feeble and day-wearied sun . . .

In the third act of *Macbeth*, when Macbeth has planned
the murder of Banquo, we have these lines:

Light thickens; and the crow
Makes wing to th' rooky wood;
Good things of Day begin to droop and drowse . . .

If I claim that the first of these extracts merely embellishes the particular situation [5], but that the second forms part of a larger pattern that lies behind the plot and the characters, on what grounds should I base my distinction? The lines from Macbeth are of course more compressed and more striking: 'light *thickens*' has an element of surprise which is lacking in the trope about night's 'black contagious breath'. And in the two and a half lines from *Macbeth* there is more *going on* than in the three lines from *King John*. Not only is the coming on of night vividly evoked, and with it a sensation of moral torpor, but the enclosed image of the crow returning to its nest introduces an extra vibration as the murderer momentarily follows its tranquil customary flight—as customary and secure as the building and breeding of the temple-haunting martlets [6]. And this, of course, is not all. In *Macbeth* previous images of darkness and of torpor have helped to determine the way in which we receive the quoted passage when it comes. Yet—and this brings me to my main point—if *King John* were full of images similar to the one I have quoted I should not feel that there was a significance in that play beyond the significance of its overt political theme. You cannot discuss imagery apart from the living tissue of which it forms a part. *King John* is a good play, containing some admirably vigorous poetry; but the kind of attention that its poetry demands is qualitatively different from the kind of attention demanded by the poetry of *Macbeth*. And the level at which meanings take place in poetry is determined by the kind and degree of activity that the poetry—the whole play—calls for on the part of the reader. Not only is the verse of *Macbeth* more fluid, more vivid and compressed than the

18

verse of *King John*, the mind of the reader or spectator is more fully activated, and activated in different ways. The compression, the thick clusters of imagery (with rapidly changing metaphors completely superseding the similes and drawn-out figures to be found in the earlier plays), the surprising juxtapositions, the over-riding of grammar, and the shifts and overlapping of meanings—all these, demanding an unusual liveliness of attention, force the reader to respond with the whole of his active imagination.

It is only when the mind of the reader is thoroughly 'roused and awakened'[7], that meanings from below the level of 'plot' and 'character' take form as a living structure. If that structure of meaning seems especially closely connected with recurring and inter-related imagery, that is not because possible associations and recurrences are puzzled out by the intellect, but because the mind at a certain pitch of activity and responsiveness combines the power of focusing lucidly on what is before it with an awareness of before and after, sensing the whole in the part, and with a triumphant energy relating part to part in a living whole. But it is only in relation to that larger all-embracing meaning—determined by the 'plain sense' of what is said, and by its overtones, by the dramatic situation and the progress of the action, by symbols and by the interplay of different attitudes embodied in the different persons of the drama—it is only in relation to this total meaning that the imagery, or any other component that may be momentarily isolated, takes on its full significance. We only hear Shakespeare's deeper meanings when we listen with the whole of ourselves.

2

At this point we may remind ourselves that modern Shakespeare scholarship offers some support to the plea (implicit in the best of recent Shakespeare criticism) that we should give to Shakespeare's plays a particular kind of attention, that we should listen to the whole orchestration and seek our meanings there, not simply picking out the more obvious tunes. Findings of the last thirty years or so concerning the Elizabethan public theatres, the Elizabethan audiences, and the conventions and traditions of Elizabethan drama suggest that the conditions under which Shakespeare wrote encouraged—or at least allowed for—an active concentration on poetry. There is no need here to go into these matters in detail, but I should like to say a word in passing about the general influence of Shakespeare's audience and Shakespeare's stage on his dramatic structures.

If, leaving aside the private theatres, we consider the audience as a whole at, say, the Globe, we have some warrant for supposing that a capacity for active listening was not confined to the Inns of Court men. A theatre audience brings with it tastes and aptitudes formed outside the theatre. We have no means of knowing how many of Shakespeare's audience listened to his plays with ears trained by listening to sermons with some attention, or how many had undergone the verbal and rhetorical education of the schools. A not negligible number certainly had. And we do know that music flourished in Shakespeare's England and that there was a widespread participation in its performance. 'Shakespeare's art,' says Yeats, 'was public, now resounding and declamatory, now lyrical and subtle, but always public, because poetry was a part of the general life of a people who had been trained by the Church to listen to difficult words, and who sang, instead of the songs of the music-halls, many songs that are still beautiful. A man who sang "Barbara Allan" in his own house would not, as I have heard the gallery at the Lyceum Theatre, receive the love speeches of

20

Juliet with an ironical chirruping'[8]. Certainly the Globe audience was a mixed assembly

—When ended is the play, the dance and song,
A thousand townsmen, gentlemen and whores
Porters and servingmen together throng—[9]

and the theatre that catered for them had to offer a variety of attractions, which included spectacle, farce, melodrama, fireworks, dancing and fights. But all ranks enjoyed the use of an undesiccated vigorous language, and deliberate skill in listening was not (to say the least) excluded from the theatres. To attend to the simple verbal patterns of *The Spanish Tragedy* (which the actors called their get-penny) was no bad training for attending to the more complex verbal patterns of *Macbeth*.

As for the actual conditions of stage performance: although we are perhaps less certain than we thought we were about some important details, we do know a good deal about the Elizabethan public theatres [10]; and what we know may be summed up by saying that the stage setting allowed only moderate scope for any latent drive towards naturalism or realism as understood by our theatre-going grandfathers. Some of the elements of convention—the 'bed thrust forth' to indicate a change of scene, or the 'roll'd bullet heard To say, it thunders'— were crude enough; but what the stage lost in sophistication and elegance (if it was a loss) was amply compensated by the opportunity offered for a flexible stagecraft. The ways in which Shakespeare took such abundant advantage of the opportunities for speed, continuity, contrast and general flexibility of handling have been brilliantly demonstrated by Granville-Barker in his *Prefaces to Shakespeare*. But it is to a special aspect of these matters that I want to draw attention here. Yeats, in his essay on 'Certain Noble Plays of Japan', says of a Japanese dancer: 'There, where no studied lighting, no stage picture made an artificial world, he was able, as he rose from the floor, where he had been sitting cross-legged, or as he threw out an arm, to recede from us into a more powerful life. Because that separation was achieved by human means alone, he receded, but to inhabit as it were the deeps of the mind.' No Elizabethan plays achieved or aimed at a formalism of that kind. But by a happy combination of circumstances some degree of formalism was inevitable. And the advantages of formalism, for dramatist and spectators, are apparent if we call to mind the extreme of naturalistic illusion provided by the cinema. We may instance the Laurence Olivier film of *Hamlet*. It was a good film, as films go, but no one who knew Shakespeare could fail to be impressed by the thinness of effect achieved by the obtrusiveness of the medium. Not only was the mind distracted by the lace of Hamlet's collar or the precariousness of his perch when speaking the 'To be, or not to be' soliloquy, the photographic realism inhibited (for me at all events) any but the crudest response. When Hamlet rejected Ophelia (knocked her down in fact), the camera's insistence on that slim sobbing figure on the stairs produced a lump in the throat that was not, I think, cathartic. Dissipation and distraction, in short, do not allow the deeps of the mind to be stirred. There is a point beyond which naturalism in art defeats its presumed aim of richness and density, and makes simply for thinness and superficiality. The Elizabethan dramatists had no coherent and explicit body of conventions, and few of them submitted to any self-denying ordinance when opportunities for a naive realism offered; but some degree of convention other than the naturalistic convention with which we are most familiar there was bound to be. And for a great artist the advantage of a non-naturalistic convention is that it favours that concentration by which he achieves the depth and activity of response at which art may be said to aim. When we claim that the essential structure of Shakespearean tragedy is poetic we at least do no violence to Shakespeare the Elizabethan dramatist.

We return therefore to what I have already said about the poetry of the greater plays and the kind of activity that it calls for if we are to meet it fully. The reader knows that what he has to deal with is not statement poetically embellished, from which the metaphors and figures could be subtracted leaving the meaning more or less intact, but with a poetry that is profoundly exploratory, that evokes what it seeks to define, and in which the implicit evaluation of experience is entirely dependent on the fulness of evocation [11]. In responding to that poetry we find that we are dealing with certain themes that shape themselves into a developing pattern. These are not 'abstract themes', 'philosophical concepts', or 'bare general propositions'; they represent a set or slant of interest that springs from and engages the concern of the personality as a whole; and although that, in turn, is far from being simply a concern for *this* man in *this* action— for it has to do with fundamental and lasting aspects of the human situation that are focused in the given case—it is only through the particular action, the precise articulation of a work of art, that it can be clarified and brought to expression. It is the artist's 'passion for the special case' that allows us, his readers, to reach and respond to universal truths.

3

The Shakespearean themes that, in the chapters that follow, I want to discuss can be indicated by such words as: time and change, appearance and reality, the fear of death and the fear of life, the meanings of nature, the meanings of relationship. Such abstract words of course tell us little about the plays in their rich concreteness, and we can only justify their use if we regard them solely as pointers. What they point towards is an organization of experience so living and complex that when we are engaged in it, living it to the full extent of our powers, we have no need of token definitions. It is only later, when we wish to give others some account of the experience to which we have responded—or, better, the experience that we have undergone—that we say, hesitatingly, 'It was about some such matters as this. Look!' It is only with this qualification that I speak of disengaging certain themes in some of Shakespeare's greater plays. And as I suggested at the end of the last section of this preliminary stocktaking, we shall be concerned not with flat statement—of a kind that can be summarized or extracted—but with generative power. Everything in fact depends on the depth at which we meet what Shakespeare offers. It is because his work incites to this active collaboration that at different stages of our lives we find different meanings, at different levels (though the new meanings do not necessarily supersede the old), and that reading Shakespeare is a perpetual discovery of ourselves. Great poetry has this in common with great moral teaching. 'The wisest of the Ancients', said Blake in his famous letter to Dr Trusler, 'consider'd what was not too Explicit as the fittest for Instruction, because it rouzes the faculties to act'.

To claim to perceive some part of the pattern, therefore, is to acknowledge that there are other ways of looking at the plays which also make sense and that 'interpretation' is a risky business: there is a 'liberty of interpreting' and truth is no man's particular property. Yet a claim to see something of a pattern may justifiably be made, and the credentials of any such claim are to be found in the extent to which it establishes coherence among a wide range of promptings that qualified readers are likely to admit as being there, in the plays. What the critic as interpreter says, in effect, is—Here is a pattern of development that makes sense: it is not the only pattern, for what we see depends partly at least on the set of our own interests, and different generations, different individuals, ask different questions of any work of art. But I believe that the themes I offer for your consideration are 'there' to this extent, that your provisional assent to them will help you towards that point, beyond 'appreciation', where you see the works in question not as isolated facts of experience, but as parts of a pattern unified 'by one significant, consistent, and developing personality'[12].

Some such claim is implicit in the pages that follow. The themes that I have been interested to trace are not, of course, parts of a prearranged pattern. They emerge from the plays because Shakespeare was trying not merely to represent 'life' but to make sense of it, to find meaning and significance. They represent answers— or attempts at answers—to urgent questions, and are, to that extent, philosophical. They do not tell the whole story of Shakespeare's development, for Shakespeare's genius was indeed many-sided, but I think that they lie near the heart of it.

CHAPTER II

The Public World: First Observations

WE no longer think of the young Shakespeare as an untutored genius, owing all to 'nature' and little to 'art'; recent scholarship has reversed the fairly widespread assumption that he was 'unlearned', and we see the early plays as deliberate exercises in established literary modes[1]. They are far enough from being merely that—even *Titus Andronicus*, with its literary and derived horrors, points forward to the preoccupation with a truly appalling inhumanity that culminates in *King Lear*—but there is a sense in which they derive not from direct observation and experience but from books. It is of course impossible to make a rigid distinction between 'literature' and 'experience'; what a man reads, if he has his wits about him, is part of his experience. Yet when we consider the early stages of Shakespeare's progress what we see most clearly is a two-fold development: the 'art' is increasingly sure, but it is an art that more and more is nourished and informed by life itself. Reality breaks in—as it does in *Love's Labour's Lost*, in Berowne's praise of love and the learning it brings—

> Learning is but an adjunct to ourself,
> And where we are our learning likewise is,

in his forswearing of affectation and pedantry ('Taffeta phrases, silken terms precise'), and indeed in the whole comic and delightful demonstration of the superiority of 'nature' to what is merely wilful and contrived: and there is an assured mockery of literary convention in the songs of Spring and Winter at the play's end.

'Realism' however means many things. There is certainly a progress from the more literary and conventional to representation springing from a clear-eyed confrontation of things as they are, of human beings as they are. But such phrases only serve our turn when we have asked questions about them. When we speak of things as they are, of people as they are, what do we mean? Well, we mean to start with what a sharpened common sense, an awareness of motives and of the way things hang together, show them to be. Yet it is still elementary (though not on that account unnecessary) to remind ourselves that behind the real in this sense—real as opposed to conventional or make-believe or literary or derivative— there are depths and complexities to which common sense fails to penetrate and of which the mere 'realist' is oblivious. Of these disturbing depths Shakespeare, being a poet, became more and more aware. Even in the early plays, where an increasing realism in its simplest sense is the most obvious sign of a fast developing maturity, this awareness is present, marked sometimes by a particular note or quality in the poetry, sometimes by the suggestion of feelings or reflections that run counter to what we have taken to be the mood of a play. In *Richard III* Clarence's dream stands out from what surrounds it not only because of the way in which it insists on the pains of conscience, but because, in more elusive ways, it points forward to Shakespeare's later sea-poetry in *Pericles* and *The Tempest*, and perhaps because of some premonitory sense in Shakespeare himself that he was about to sound deep waters. In *Love's Labour's Lost* the penance imposed on Berowne—

> You shall this twelvemonth term, from day to day,
> Visit the speechless sick, and still converse
> With groaning wretches—

lightly as it is taken, is still a reminder of a world that con-

27

tains much more than wooing, word-play and high spirits. And in *Romeo and Juliet*, deliberately artificial as so much of the love poetry is, there are passages as far beyond the powers of shrewd observation as they are from mere poeticising.

> I am no pilot; yet, wert thou as far
> As that vast shore wash'd with the farthest sea,
> I would adventure for such merchandise.

> My bounty is as boundless as the sea,
> My love as deep; the more I give to thee,
> The more I have, for both are infinite.

Such things point forward to much that is to come; in the early plays it is equally important to notice that they are there, and that they are exceptional: it is first through 'realism' that the progress lies. Meanwhile we may remind ourselves that the genuine sense of the mysterious depths of human experience, the genuine sense of a deeper reality, is, in literature, most truly grasped by the writer who is most firmly based on the actuality of every day: we recall how sharp and clear is Dante's vision of the everyday and familiar world.

With the possible exception of *Romeo and Juliet* all the more significant of Shakespeare's early plays deal with public themes: their protagonists are, ostensibly, figures from history, in actuality representative figures from the world of great affairs. It is in this area of human experience that Shakespeare made some of his keenest observations, and the interest that determined the choice of subject for —probably—his earliest plays remained active throughout his career. When we look at the whole sequence of the political plays (for this, rather than 'History plays, English and Roman', seems the best description of them) we see a steady deepening of the vision and an increasingly close relationship with work that is not formally historical or political. The connexions are close and intricate. In the public world the conflicts are no simpler, the contradictions no less deeply rooted, than in more intimate relationships or within the individual himself. Indeed the distinguishing mark of Shakespeare's handling of political actions is the clarity with which he sees them, not in terms of 'politics' (that word which, perhaps as much as any, is responsible for simplification and distortion in our thinking) but in terms of their causes in human fears and desires and of particular human consequences. His interest in politics was of a kind that led, inevitably, beyond them, and the insights that made possible *Coriolanus* were developed outside the bounds of a merely political concern[2]. This, however, is to anticipate. All I wish to remark here is that the public world of the early plays is not, so to speak, felt from within, but it is a world that is keenly *observed*. For our present purposes both the negative and the positive implications of this are important.

In the first four plays on English history—the three parts of *Henry VI* and *Richard III*—the conventional and formal mode (history moralized on the Tudor pattern)[3] is increasingly qualified by reality breaking in. To say this does not of course mean that there is a simple progress from 'convention' to naturalism; it means that within the formal pattern Shakespeare can make us see and feel the human actuality. A small but significant example is the scene in *Richard III* (III, vii) in which Gloucester, suitably discovered at his devotions between a couple of bishops, pretends reluctance to take the crown, offered to him as the result of a carefully rigged meeting at the Guildhall. The comedy of the scene is simple enough, but it is entirely serious, and it lies in the contrast of what may be called the newspaper-headline view of events and what we know is the truth of the matter[4]. Or again, in *2 Henry VI*, there is the well-known scene of Cade's oration to his men.

CADE. Be brave then; for your captain is brave, and vows reformation. There shall be in England seven halfpenny loaves sold for a penny; the three-hooped pot shall have ten hoops; and I will make it felony to drink small beer. All the realm shall be in common, and in Cheapside shall my palfrey go to grass. And when I am king, as king I will be,—

ALL. God save your majesty!

CADE. I thank you good people: there shall be no money; all shall eat and drink on my score; and I will apparel them all in one livery, that they may agree like brothers, and worship me their lord.

(IV. ii)

The point is not simply that Cade is a 'character', whereas Iden, say, is a type figure. That Shakespeare did not so cast him, as a mere representative of 'commotion' (III. i. 358), was not entirely because Cade offered an opportunity for a bit of incidental comedy; we may fairly assume it was because he could not suppress his interest in the actuality of the demagogue, in the private motives and muddles that at any time may make their impact— transient or more lasting—on the public world. Much of *King Henry VI* is, as it were, action seen at a distance—as children see history, or as most of us tend to see world affairs. When Shakespeare alters the focus (and this is a dramatic device that he was to use repeatedly later), we have a close-up view of what we had taken to be a pageant: history and politics begin to appear differently. And it is in the development of a particular manner of speech that the pressure of life makes itself felt.

This new kind of interest, demanding a new use of words, centres on the figure of Richard of Gloucester, who in the Third Part of *Henry VI* announces his intention of setting the murderous Machiavel to school. *Richard III* is still to some extent a political morality play in which events—like some of the speeches—are rather stiffly formalized and patterned. But Richard himself isn't simply a morality figure—Cunning Craft or Policy. The way he speaks—the way Shakespeare makes him speak— relates him directly to a world that is seen and felt close at hand. In *Henry VI* Shakespeare uses more than one style, but the following, from the Second Part (II. vi), is not uncharacteristic of that play: the speaker is the mortally wounded Clifford.

> The common people swarm like summer flies;
> And whither fly the gnats but to the sun?
> And who shines now but Henry's enemies?
> O Phoebus, hadst thou never given consent
> That Phaëthon should check thy fiery steeds,
> Thy burning car never had scorched the earth!
> And, Henry, hadst thou sway'd as kings should do,
> Or as thy father and his father did,
> Giving no ground unto the house of York,
> They never then had sprung like summer flies;
> I and ten thousand in this luckless realm
> Had left no mourning widows for our death;
> And thou this day hadst kept thy chair in peace.
> For what does cherish weeds but gentle air?
> And what makes robbers bold but too much lenity?
> Bootless are plaints, and cureless are my wounds;
> No way to fly, nor strength to hold out flight:
> The foe is merciless, and will not pity;
> For at their hands I have deserved no pity.

We have only to put beside this a passage from the open-ing soliloquy of *Richard III* to see how rapidly Shake-speare's resources are developing, and in what direction.

> Grim-visag'd War hath smooth'd his wrinkled front;
> And now, instead of mounting barbed steeds,
> To fright the souls of fearful adversaries,
> He capers nimbly in a lady's chamber,
> To the lascivious pleasing of a lute.

31

But I, that am not shap'd for sportive tricks,
Nor made to court an amorous looking-glass;
I, that am rudely stamp'd and want love's majesty,
To strut before a wanton ambling nymph;
I, that am curtail'd of this fair proportion,
Cheated of feature by dissembling Nature,
Deform'd, unfinish'd, sent before my time
Into this breathing world, scarce half made up,
And that so lamely and unfashionably,
That dogs bark at me as I halt by them;
Why, I, in this weak piping time of peace,
Have no delight to pass away the time,
Unless to spy my shadow in the sun,
And descant on mine own deformity.
And therefore, since I cannot prove a lover,
To entertain these fair well-spoken days,
I am determined to prove a villain . . .

Of this speech Mr Traversi says, 'Although a certain stilted quality survives in the movement of the verse . . . the general effect is remarkably concise and pointed. Richard's state of mind is conveyed primarily through a series of sharp visual touches directly expressed—the vision of himself as "strutting" ludicrously before a "wanton, ambling nymph", as being "barked at" by the dogs as he passes before them, as "spying" his misshapen shadow in the sun. . . . In this way, by making envy the vehicle for a criticism felt, by its very directness, not to be altogether unjustified, the speaker is humanized, transformed from the abstract incarnation of a traditional vice exploited for melodramatic effect into something like a person'[5]. It would be difficult to improve on this account of a realistic manner that, in this play, we associate especially with Richard. There are his characteristically terse asides ('But yet I run before my horse to market'), and even the formal oration to his army before Bosworth has a colloquial vividness.

Remember whom you are to cope withal;
A sort of vagabonds, rascals, and runaways,
A scum of Bretons, and base lackey peasants, . . .
And who doth lead them but a paltry fellow,
Long kept in Bretagne at our mother's cost?
A milk-sop, one that never in his life
Felt so much cold as over shoes in snow!
Let's whip these stragglers o'er the seas again . . .
If we conquer'd, let men conquer us,
And not these bastard Bretons, whom our fathers
Have in their own land beaten, bobb'd and thump'd.
(v. iii. 316-35)

In the presentation of Richard, then, there is a new psychological interest[6]. (It is significant that Shakespeare drew on More's vivid and dramatic presentation in his *Life of Richard III*[7].) But it is as the Machiavel—not the merely theatrical Machiavel, but the a-moral political 'realist'—that Shakespeare is primarily interested in him. Or perhaps we should say that the interest in the Machiavel, the public figure, is inseparable from the psychological interest in the man with a grudge against the world.

I have no brother, I am like no brother;
And this word 'love', which greybeards call divine,
Be resident in men like one another
And not in me: I am myself alone.[8]

As Mr Danby has pointed out[9], this speech of Richard's, when he has killed Henry VI, looks forward to some of Shakespeare's profounder searchings of the human situation. Meanwhile we may simply notice that in the presentation of Richard Shakespeare is developing an idiom and manner in which the political world can be seen directly, can be brought closer to what the audience directly knows, or can be brought to see, of men and affairs.

This manner is brilliantly developed in *King John*. There is a new activity in the descriptive passages, as in

C 33

the well-known account of the spread of anxious rumour
(IV. ii. 185-202) or in the Bastard's defiance of the
Dauphin's troops.

> That hand which had the strength, even at your
>   door,
> To cudgel you and make you take the hatch,
> To dive like buckets in concealed wells,
> To crouch in litter of your stable planks,
> To lie like pawns lock'd up in chests and trunks,
> To hug with swine, to seek sweet safety out
> In vaults and prisons, and to thrill and shake
> Even at the crying of your nation's crow,
> Thinking his voice an armed Englishman;
> Shall that victorious hand be feebled here,
> That in your chambers gave you chastisement?
>   (v. ii. 137-47)

As is plain from these lines, it is a manner particularly
suited for the purposes of mockery or satire, and it is the
Bastard's especial rôle to act as a solvent of all that is
high-flown and exaggerated, whether it is literary affectation (II. i. 504-9) or social pretension:

>   Now your traveller,
> He and his toothpick at my worship's mess,
> And when my knightly stomach is sufficed,
> Why then I suck my teeth and catechize
> My picked man of countries: 'My dear sir,'
> Thus, leaning on mine elbow, I begin,
> 'I shall beseech you'—that is question now;
> And then comes answer like an Absey book:
> 'O sir,' says answer, 'at your best command;
> At your employment; at your service, sir:'
> 'No, sir,' says question, 'I, sweet sir, at yours:'
> And so, ere answer knows what question would,
> Saving in dialogue of compliment,
> And talking of the Alps and Apennines,
> The Pyrenean and the river Po,

It draws toward supper in conclusion so.
But this is worshipful society . . . .

(I. i. 189-205)

This last passage has a particular significance: by a variety of devices, including exaggerated gesture ('Thus, leaning on mine elbow, I begin . . .') and sardonic alliteration ('The Pyrenean and the river Po'), 'worshipful society' is shown from the standpoint of an outsider, but (there is neither fuss nor bitterness in the satire) one who clearly *belongs* elsewhere. As I have said in another connexion, his idiom, references and manner relate him directly to the local world, where 'St George, that swinged the dragon . . . sits on his horse back at mine hostess' door', a world where observation is direct and comment forthright[10].

The world into which the Bastard is introduced is the world of statecraft—the Renaissance world, where 'policy', by the end of the sixteenth century, had acquired its sinister implication. The precepts of Machiavelli's *The Prince* had of course been followed, if not formulated, before the sixteenth century; but it was not without reason that the Elizabethans saw in 'the Machiavel' a portent. In economic affairs, in national politics and international relations, perhaps more than ever before, men were becoming aware of what could be achieved by the will directed to 'rational'—that is, clearly defined—ends. In other words, there was an increasing preoccupation with the problem of power, especially of power divorced from conscience. In *Richard III* the question had been debated by the two murderers of Clarence.

FIRST MURDERER. Where's thy conscience now?
SECOND MURDERER. O, in the Duke of Gloucester's purse.
FIRST MURDERER. When he opens his purse to give us our reward, thy conscience flies out.

35

SECOND MURDERER. 'Tis no matter, let it go: there's few or none will entertain it.

FIRST MURDERER. What if it come to thee again?

SECOND MURDERER. I'll not meddle with it: it makes a man a coward . . . 'Tis a blushing shamefast spirit, that mutinies in a man's bosom; it fills a man full of obstacles . . . it is turn'd out of towns and cities for a dangerous thing; and every man that means to live well endeavours to trust to himself and to live without it. (I. iv. 125-42)

And lest this should be thought irrelevant to the main theme Richard himself was made to reveal that the basic assumption of power politics is the same as the Second Murderer's.

Conscience is but a word that cowards use,
Devis'd at first to keep the strong in awe;
Our strong arms be our conscience, swords our law!
(v. iii. 310-12)

The rulers in *King John* are not quite so explicit. When the contending parties meet before Angiers both the King of France and the Duke of Austria profess lofty and disinterested motives; and even John, whose 'strong possession' of the crown is much more than his 'right' (I. i. 40), can adopt at times a lofty religious tone. The upshot of the meeting of the kings is a marriage alliance determined purely by 'policy', and it is this that gives the Bastard his opportunity to comment directly on the political action.

Mad world! mad kings! mad composition!
John, to stop Arthur's title in the whole,
Hath willingly departed with a part:
And France, whose armour conscience buckled on,
Whom zeal and charity brought to the field
As God's own soldier, rounded in the ear
With that same purpose-changer, that sly devil,
That broker, that still breaks the pate of faith,

That daily break-vow, he that wins of all,
Of kings, of beggars, old men, young men, maids,
Who, having no external thing to lose
But the word 'maid', cheats the poor maid of that,
That smooth-faced gentleman, tickling Commodity,
Commodity, the bias of the world,
The world, who of itself is peised well,
Made to run even upon even ground,
Till this advantage, this vile-drawing bias,
This sway of motion, this Commodity,
Makes it take head from all indifferency,
From all direction, purpose, course, intent:
And this same bias, this Commodity,
This bawd, this broker, this all-changing word,
Clapp'd on the outward eye of fickle France,
Hath drawn him from his own determined aid,
From a resolved and honourable war,
To a most base and vile-concluded peace.
And why rail I on this Commodity?
But for because he hath not woo'd me yet . . .
Since kings break faith upon commodity,
Gain be my lord, for I will worship thee.

(II. i. 561-88)

The Bastard's profession of self-interest—judging by his subsequent conduct—is not to be taken at its face value, but there is no doubt that his speech as a whole, with its racy colloquial turns and shrewd realism, is the pivot on which the play turns. Indeed, so far as any one speech can, it sums up Shakespeare's view of the public world at this stage of his career.

King John, it is true, is not an entirely satisfactory play. At the end the English lords, who have revolted because of what they consider John's crime against Arthur, on learning that the Dauphin intends to double-cross them return to their allegiance—'even to our ocean, to our great King John', who has been shown as anything but great; and the action is rounded off with a simple patriotic appeal—

> This England never did, nor never shall,
> Lie at the proud foot of a conqueror,
> But when it first did help to wound itself.
> ... Nought shall make us rue,
> If England to itself do rest but true.

But the play as a whole is anything but a simple patriotic play; nor is it merely a play about past history; it is a play about international politics, which are seen with complete realism through the eyes of the Bastard. In the plays that follow, Shakespeare was to find subtler means of expressing and enforcing judgment on the presented action; and he was never again to sum up with the simple obviousness of the speech on Commodity. But the Bastard represents something fundamental in Shakespeare's outlook on the world; he represents the habit of looking at things directly, of cutting through pretence and getting behind the words that disguise reality. In the greater plays on social and political themes, Shakespeare takes a situation, an attitude, an idea, and asks, *What does this mean*, in terms of specific human causes and consequences?[11]

In the First Part of *King Henry IV* the question that Shakespeare is asking is, What does it mean to use force for political ends, to seek and keep power? The facts of the situation—I mean the dramatic facts, not any that may be brought in from historical knowledge extraneous to the play—are clear. Henry Bolingbroke is a usurping king, who is now meeting the consequences of usurpation in precisely the way that was foretold in *Richard II*[12]. But we are concerned not only with a succession of 'facts' but with interpretation and judgment—and judgment has to do with the way in which, at particular places within a developing context, we give or refuse imaginative assent to the varied attitudes or life-directions, revealed through the spoken word, whose struggle and interaction constitute the drama. It is certain that the rebels, the Northumberland faction, do not enlist our sympathy. Indeed they are often presented satirically, as in the comedy of their first meeting, where Worcester and Hotspur take turns in deflating each other's rhetoric:

> WORCESTER. . . . And now I will unclasp a secret book,
>   And to your quick-conceiving discontents
>   I'll read you matter deep and dangerous,
>   As full of peril and adventurous spirit
>   As to o'er-walk a current roaring loud
>   On the unsteadfast footing of a spear.
> HOTSPUR. If he fall in, good night! or sink or swim . . .
>   (I. iii. 188-94)

In spite of the moral indignation they can direct against Bolingbroke, there is really no pretence that they are setting out to right a wrong. They simply stand for factional interests whose determined pursuit is bound to lead to further bloodshed and disorder—to 'pellmell havoc and confusion' (v. i. 82). Worcester, as spokesman of the faction, may complain to Henry of 'unkind usage . . . violation of all faith and troth' (v. i. 69-70), but it is Worcester who lets us know that the public and diplomatic colouring is no more than that—

> For well you know we of the offering side
> Must keep aloof from strict arbitrement,
> And stop all sight-holes, every loop from whence
> The eye of reason may pry in upon us;
>   (IV. i. 69-72)

and it is he who conceals the king's 'liberal and kind offer' of peace before Shrewsbury:

> It is not possible, it cannot be,
> The king should keep his word in loving us;
> He will suspect us still, and find a time

To punish this offence in other faults:
Suspicion all our lives shall be stuck full of eyes;
For treason is but trusted like the fox . . .

(v. ii. 4-9)

Yet the rebels' view of how the king came to his throne—and they revert to it often enough—is not far from what Henry himself admits. Hotspur speaks of 'murderous subornation' (I. iii. 163), of a hypocritical pretence of righting wrongs, whereas Henry speaks of 'necessity',

. . . necessity so bow'd the state,
That I and greatness were compell'd to kiss,

(Part II, III. i. 73-4)

but even he admits to his son that he used considerable astuteness to 'pluck allegiance from men's hearts' (III. ii. 39 ff.), and, as he says on his death-bed,

God knows, my son,
By what by-paths and indirect crook'd ways
I met this crown.

(Part II, IV. v. 183-5)

The 'necessity' to which he submitted has its own laws, and although there is the accent of sincerity whenever Henry reflects on the condition of England—'my poor kingdom, sick with civil blows!' (Part II, IV. v. 133)—or urges the need for peace, he is caught in a chain of consequences from which he cannot escape,

For all my reign hath been but as a scene
Acting that argument . . .

(Part II, IV. v. 197-8)

What we have in 1 *Henry IV* therefore is a realistic portrayal of the ways of the world and an insistent questioning of the values by which its great men live—with a consequent ironic contrast between public profession and the actuality. The questioning centres on the nature of 'honour'. Shakespeare does not say that honour is unreal, a mere abstract word with which men hide reality from themselves: he simply points out—that is, the play has the effect of pointing out—that whether honour means much or little depends on the person using it. Hotspur is of course the chief exponent of Honour in the conventional sense, and the forced rhetoric with which he presents his ideal is comment enough.

> By heaven, methinks it were an easy leap,
> To pluck bright honour from the pale-faced moon,
> Or dive into the bottom of the deep,
> Where fathom-line could never touch the ground,
> And pluck up drowned honour by the locks;
> So he that doth redeem her thence might wear
> Without corrival all her dignities.
>
> (I. iii. 201-7)

But Hotspur, fundamentally immature as he is in his aggressive self-assertion (as also, incidentally, in his relations with his wife), is not only taken seriously by the other characters, as such people have to be, he is accorded respect. For Henry he is 'a son who is the theme of honour's tongue' (I. i. 81); and although Prince Hal can produce an amusing skit on the swashbuckling hero—'he that kills me some six or seven dozen of Scots at a breakfast, washes his hands, and says to his wife "Fie upon this quiet life! I want work." ' (II. iv. 102-5)—Hal too accepts the conventions:

> Percy is but my factor, good my lord,
> To engross up glorious deeds on my behalf;
> And I will call him to so strict account,
> That he shall render every glory up . . .
>
> (III. ii. 147-50)

Honour, then, is simply military glory—a prerogative of the nobleman who can afford to forget the humbler realities of warfare.

41

But the play as a whole does not allow us to forget them. The element of unreality in the world of the military and political leaders—their failure to take enough into account—is made plain in various ways. There is the persistent imagery of physical violence which throughout the play reminds us that warfare is not simply a form of sport,—

> And as the soldiers bore dead bodies by,
> He call'd them untaught knaves, unmannerly,
> To bring a slovenly unhandsome corse
> Betwixt the wind and his nobility.
>
> (I. iii. 42-5)

There is deliberate juxtaposition, with an effect of implicit critical comment, as when Vernon's description of the Prince of Wales and his comrades in arms

> —Glittering in golden coats, like images;
> As full of spirit as the month of May—
>
> (IV. i. 100-1)

is followed, first, by Hotspur's invocation of Mars 'up to the ears in blood' (IV. i. 112-17), and then, almost without a pause, by Falstaff's account of the military operations whereby a hundred and fifty scarecrows are led to take their part in the same 'glorious day' (III. ii. 133).

> I have misused the king's press damnably. I have got, in exchange of a hundred and fifty soldiers, three hundred and odd pounds. I press me none but good house-holders, yeomen's sons; inquire me out con-tracted bachelors . . . I pressed me none but such toasts-and-butter, with hearts in their bellies no bigger than pins'-heads, and they have bought out their services; and now my whole charge consists of ancients, corporals, lieutenants, gentlemen of companies, slaves as ragged as Lazarus in the painted cloth, where the glutton's dogs licked his sores; and such indeed as were never soldiers . . . and such have I, to fill up the

42

rooms of them that have bought out their services, that you would think that I had a hundred and fifty tattered prodigals lately come from swine-keeping, from eating draff and husks. (IV. ii. 12-36)

In short, within the space of some eighty lines, we have successive glimpses of the chivalric, the barbaric ('all hot and bleeding'), and the completely unheroic aspects of war: Shakespeare does not say that one is 'truer' than another, but Falstaff's 'pitiful rascals'—'good enough to toss; food for powder' (IV. ii. 66)—are, after all, part of the setting in which the nobles expect to purchase honour.

It is of course from Falstaff, whose obvious comic function combines with a more serious rôle, that the main explicit criticism comes. He may be in part the personification of Misrule from whom it is the Prince's business to escape, but clearly he cannot be reduced to a morality abstraction. It is impossible to think of him, as Hal tends to do, simply as 'blown Jack' or 'guts'—his mind moves more quickly than that of anyone else in the play—but over against Hotspur's abstraction, 'honour', he does represent the life of the body, intent on its own preservation and the satisfaction of its instincts, and his philosophy is summed up in the famous soliloquy before Shrewsbury.

> Well, 'tis no matter; honour pricks me on. Yea, but how if honour prick me off when I come on? how then? Can honour set to a leg? no: or an arm? no: or take away the grief of a wound? no. Honour hath no skill in surgery, then? no. What is honour? a word. What is in that word honour? what is that honour? air. A trim reckoning! Who hath it? he that died o' Wednesday, Doth he feel it? no. Doth he hear it? no. 'Tis insensible, then? yea, to the dead. But will it not live with the living? no. Why? detraction will not suffer it. Therefore I'll none of it. Honour is a mere scutcheon; and so ends my catechism. (V. i. 129-41)

Shakespeare's philosophy, to be sure, is not Falstaff's. Falstaff too is presented critically, as 'riot and dishonour', and even in Part I there is enough to prevent us from taking him (as we take the Bastard) for an entirely reliable commentator. Nevertheless there is a sense in which Falstaff is, as Middleton Murry calls him, 'a triumphant particular crystallization of the general element' [13], and through him—to change the metaphor—the pervasive ironic vision comes to its sharpest focus. It is largely because Falstaff is in the play that we are able to see how flawed and unsatisfactory is the public world.

In *Henry V*, in *Julius Caesar* and, later, in *Coriolanus*, Shakespeare was to continue his exploration of the public world and its tragic contradictions, and of the rôle of the Governor. But between *1 Henry IV* and *Henry V* Shakespeare wrote *2 Henry IV*; and the Second Part of *King Henry IV* is a different kind of play from the first Part. There is certainly continuity, but there is also a new direction of interest and the action is contrived for new purposes: there is a greater involvement of the dramatist in his fable. The meaning of that involvement will from now on be our main concern, and for that reason it seems important to emphasize once more the realism—the detached observation and irony—that has been briefly illustrated in this chapter. This shrewd understanding of men in their political and public aspects and relations (not 'disillusioned', because that implies an attitude to the self quite foreign to Shakespeare, but certainly without illusions) was an essential condition of Shakespeare's exploration of experiences that come to each man simply as individual man in his more directly personal life and relationships. It meant that the inwardness was to be something utterly different from the results of an engrossed introspection.

CHAPTER III

Time's Subjects: The Sonnets and
King Henry IV, Part II

THE Shakespeare of early maturity—the Shakespeare newly emerged from the apprentice period of *Henry VI* and *Titus Andronicus* and *The Taming of the Shrew*—possessed in an eminent degree a quality without which no poet ever wrote poetry. I mean simply an energetic consciousness and an appetite for life: a zest that displayed itself in verbal fluency and virtuosity, a readiness to experiment, a capacity for intellectual excitement, and a lively observation of the varied forms of nature and humanity. This buoyancy is obvious, and without it Shakespeare would not have become the great poet that he is. But buoyancy alone never made a great poet, let alone a great tragic poet. Great poetry demands a willingness to meet, experience and contemplate all that is most deeply disturbing in our common fate. The sense of life's tragic issues comes to different men in different ways. One of the ways in which it came to Shakespeare is not uncommon; it was simply a heightened awareness of what the mere passage of time does to man and all created things. There are many of the Sonnets that show the impact of time and mutability on a nature endowed with an uncommon capacity for delight. And it is surely no accident that one of the first plays in which we recognize the great Shakespeare—the Second Part of *King Henry IV* —is a play of which the controlling theme is time and change. In that play, and in the sonnets on time, we see clearly the beginning of the progress that culminates in *King Lear* and the great tragedies.

I

As everyone knows, the Sonnets contain a number of themes that seem to issue directly from the life history of the poet; and if we make a prose paraphrase of the poems in the order in which they appeared in Thorpe's edition of 1609 we can piece together a story that has a tantalizing appearance of fragmentary autobiography. There are various reasons for not finding this an entirely satisfactory procedure. One of them is that it takes no account of the close connexion between technical mastery and the degree of a writer's engagement in what he is writing about. Part of the interest the Sonnets have for us is that in them, within the limitations of a highly conventional form, we can see Shakespeare working towards power and subtlety in the use of language—a process comparable to the development of his dramatic blank verse. But they are comparatively early work and we find within them very different levels of poetic achievement. If we are seeking the themes in which Shakespeare's interests are most deeply engaged, we need to be alert to the varied potency of the language. It is only when we really accept this truism that we are in any position to decide in what ways Shakespeare followed Sidney's injunction—'Fool, said my Muse to me, look in thy heart and write'.

It is at all events clear that some, at least, of the sonnets in which the 'story' element is intrusive are among the least interesting as poetry. Sonnet XLII, for example ('That thou hast her, it is not all my grief'), which is as explicit as any concerning the mistress stolen by the friend, would very properly have been ignored if it had appeared in an anthology of anonymous verse. But if this ingenious little exercise is considered too artificial even for the purposes of elementary comparison, we may take a sonnet that, with some genuine individuality of phras-

46

ing, deals directly with a personal relationship, and put beside it another in which the 'personal' theme involves the poet in a meditation of a very different kind. Here, then, is Sonnet CII, which deals with the relationship of poet and patron, followed by Sonnet LX, which is one of many whose ostensible purpose is to promise a poetic immortality to the beloved.

My love is strengthen'd, though more weak in
    seeming;
I love not less, though less the show appear:
That love is merchandiz'd whose rich esteeming
The owner's tongue doth publish everywhere.
Our love was new, and then but in the spring,
When I was wont to greet it with my lays;
As Philomel in summer's front doth sing,
And stops her pipe in growth of riper days:
Not that the summer is less pleasant now
Than when her mournful hymns did hush the night,
But that wild music burthens every bough,
And sweets grown common lose their dear delight.
    Therefore, like her, I sometimes hold my tongue,
    Because I would not dull you with my song.

Like as the waves make towards the pebbled shore,
So do our minutes hasten to their end;
Each changing place with that which goes before,
In sequent toil all forwards do contend.
Nativity, once in the main of light,
Crawls to maturity, wherewith being crown'd,
Crooked eclipses 'gainst his glory fight,
And Time that gave doth now his gift confound.
Time doth transfix the flourish set on youth
And delves the parallels in beauty's brow,
Feeds on the rarities of nature's truth,
And nothing stands but for his scythe to mow:
    And yet to times in hope my verse shall stand,
    Praising thy worth, despite his cruel hand.

The difference in tone and manner needs no comment. Sonnet CII has, most evidently, 'the delight in richness and sweetness of sound' which Coleridge noted as one of the signs of original genius in a young poet. It is very beautiful, but the beauty is that of romantic enchantment; it asks an entirely different kind of reading from the other. Sonnet LX is urgent and forthright; there are powerful phrases, but none that tempts us to linger on a beauty that is extrinsic to the matter in hand. Shakespeare, we feel, is fully engaged in the imaginative evocation of the irreversible processes of time. If we were to try to summarize the plain sense of the poem we should have to say something like this:—'Nothing can resist the encroachments of time, which continually takes away what it gives; yet my verse shall continue to exist and to sing your praises to future generations.' But in the poetry it is the logically subordinated matter of time's action—vividly realized in the superb imagery of twelve out of the fourteen lines—that enlists our feelings, that we remember, and not the promise at the end. And this is an observation that can be generalized.

It has become a commonplace that one of the most consistently developed themes of Shakespeare's Sonnets— of those at all events in which the linguistic vitality is highest—is Time[1]. Not of course that Time's 'rage' is always the ostensible or formal subject. It is simply that whenever there is occasion to mention Time and 'nature's changing course' the theme takes possession: there is a sharpness and urgency of phrase; and however fast we hold to the thread of sense and argument, the imagery involves us in a world where

> everything that grows
> Holds in perfection but a little moment,

where

48

men as plants increase,
Cheered and check'd even by the self-same sky,
Vaunt in their youthful sap, at height decrease,
And wear their brave state out of memory,
(XV)

where, in short, 'nothing stands but for [Time's] scythe to mow'. One reason of course why Time comes into the picture at all is that many of the sonnets are about ways of defeating him—getting married and having children, or writing immortal verse, or, best of all, loving so truly that Time can make no difference. But the poet is not interested in the young patron's posterity with the same intensity of concern that is evoked by the signs of beauty's passing (consider, for example, Sonnets V, XII and XV); and even the magnificent assertion of love's independence of Time in Sonnet CXVI

—Love's not Time's fool, though rosy lips and cheeks
Within his bending sickle's compass come—

is (for me) simply an assertion, rather than a final insight to which we are compelled by that honesty of imagination which takes everything into account. The imagination of course can leap ahead of experience, though only in such a way that experience—what is intimately known—feels itself able to follow in its tracks; and both Sonnet CXVI ('Let me not to the marriage of true minds') and Sonnet CXXIV ('If my dear love were but the child of state'), and perhaps others, may be taken as pointing forward to fundamental recognitions to be found in Shakespeare's later work. But in the sequence as a whole the assurance of love's 'unknown' worth

—It is the star to every wandering bark,
Whose worth's unknown, although his height be
taken— (CXVI)

is, as yet, set over against what the imagination has made

most real: there are whole tracts of experience still to be crossed. What we feel, again and again, in those sonnets that are most powerfully alive, is the sense of Time—the 'dial's shady stealth'—summed up in unforgettable images of the changing seasons and the wasting years.

One may suppose that the early work of genius, where it is most deeply felt, must contain marked premonitions of later development; there is a basic cast of mind and there are fundamental preoccupations. Perhaps in the Sonnets 'the essential Shakespeare' is to be found in a fourfold inclination of the spirit. There is a keen and pervasive love of life—especially of all that suggests fresh and unforced latent power, including the world of nature, into which by metaphor and analogy man is so often assimilated. There is an equally keen, equally pervasive feeling for the stealthy and unimpeded undermining by Time of what the heart holds most dear:

> Since brass, nor stone, nor earth, nor boundless sea,
> But sad mortality o'er-sways their power,
> How with this rage shall beauty hold a plea
> Whose action is no stronger than a flower?
>
> (LXV)

And finally, allied with a capacity for self-searching and moral discrimination, there is a groping for some certitude to set over against the perpetual flux of things, an intimation that love alone 'stands hugely politic, That it nor grows with heat nor drowns with showers' (CXXIV).

In the Shakespearean progress all these deeply personal leanings will be richly nourished and will unfold into a pattern, a structure of meanings, far more rich and complex than can be found in the Sonnets themselves. There will be an unfailing increase of delighted observation, not only of all that is simply beautiful but, as we should expect from the early plays, of all the varied forms of life: not only of the spring and foison of the year but of every variety of living thing—the peacock that 'stalks up and down . . . a stride and a stand', the distracted tavern-keeper 'that hath no arithmetic but her brain to set down her reckoning', the vain man who 'bites his lip with a politic regard, as who should say, "There were wit in this head, and 'twould out" '[2]. At the same time, the preoccupation with mutability will become a preoccupation not only with deceitful appearances and false-seeming but with the sources of illusion in the recesses of personal life, in the distorted imagination: a preoccupation leading in recoil to a profound searching for something that, opposed to appearance and in spite of time and death, may be welcomed as reality. And when that patient passionate exploration has reached its centre there will be a marvellous celebration of values that are not only in wish but in fact 'builded far from accident'—values that are first disengaged and established by probing the varied negations of evil and false choice, and then celebrated more directly in complex dramatic symbols of renewal. From the Sonnets to *The Tempest* Shakespeare's progress as a dramatist is not to be summed up as a series of adventures of the soul; like that of all great artists it is a directed exploration. True enough, it is only when we begin to see the whole pattern that we can realize how completely Shakespeare was committed, for in each new venture there is freedom as well as commitment, and nothing could be further than these plays from the compulsive following of an idea. But the imagination has its responsibilities, and Shakespeare found his when, in a deeply personal experience, he confronted the power of Time[3].

2

In Sonnet LXIV, pondering the general instability of things, Shakespeare had instanced the shifting edges of the sea:

When I have seen the hungry ocean gain
Advantage of the kingdom of the shore,
And the firm soil win of the watery main,
Increasing store with loss and loss with store . . .

The image is repeated, with an added note of irony for men's expectation of stability, in the Second Part of *King Henry IV*:

O God! that one might read the book of fate,
And see the revolution of the times
Make mountains level, and the continent,
Weary of solid firmness, melt itself
Into the sea! and, other times, to see
The beachy girdle of the ocean
Too wide for Neptune's hips; how chances mock,
And changes fill the cup of alteration
With divers liquors![4]   (III. i. 45-53)

This, so far as any one passage can, suggests the nature of the imaginative vision that is now coming to expression in the plays. *2 Henry IV*, a tragi-comedy of human frailty, is about the varied aspects of mutability—age, disappointment and decay. The theme of 'policy' is of course continued from Part I, and sometimes it is presented with similar methods of ironic deflation; but we cannot go far into the play without becoming aware of a change of emphasis and direction, already marked indeed by the words of the dying Hotspur at Shrewsbury,

But thought's the slave of life, and life time's fool;
And time, that takes survey of all the world,
Must have a stop.

Each of the three scenes of the first act gives a particular emphasis to elements present in Part I, though largely subdued there by the brisker tone, by the high-spirited satire. Now the proportions are altered. Act I, scene i is not comic satire: it is a harsh reminder of what is involved in the hard game of power politics—the desperate resolve

('each heart being set On bloody courses . . .') and the
penalties for failure; and for some thirty lines, throughout
Northumberland's elaborate rhetoric of protestation
against ill news (I. i. 67-103), the word 'dead' (or 'death')
tolls with monotonous insistence. Now just as the
comedy of the first meeting of the conspirators in Part I
was in keeping with the Falstaffian mode that so largely
determined the tone of that play, so this scene is attuned
to the appearance of a Falstaff who seems, at first perplex-
ingly, to be both the same figure as before and yet
another: it is as though we had given a further twist to the
screw of our binoculars and a figure that we thought we
knew had appeared more sharply defined against a background that he no longer dominated. When Falstaff
enters with his page ('Sirrah, you giant, what says the
doctor to my water?'), throughout his exchange with the
Lord Chief Justice, and in his concluding soliloquy, it is
impossible to turn the almost obsessive references to age
and disease, as the references to Falstaff's corpulence are
turned in Part I, in the direction of comedy[5]. Later,
Falstaff will try again his familiar tactics of evasion—
'Peace, good Doll! do not speak like a death's-head; do
not bid me remember mine end' (II. iv. 229-30); but from
the scene of his first appearance the well-known *memento
mori*, if not—as in *The Revenger's Tragedy*—actually
present on the stage, has certainly been present to the
minds of the audience. 'Is not . . . every part about you
blasted with antiquity?'—to that question wit in its
wantonness must make what reply it can.

Scene iii, where some of the principal rebels discuss
their resources and prospects, is short but significant. As in
the preceding scenes the significance is found not in any
precisely controlled minute particulars of the poetry but
simply in a certain expansiveness and insistence at key
points; what our thoughts are directed towards is the lack

of certainty in human affairs and the consequent precariousness of those hopes that are so often referred to (seven times in sixty one lines, to be exact). Hastings is for going ahead and trusting that things will turn out well; Lord Bardolph urges caution.

> HASTINGS. But, by your leave, it never yet did hurt
> To lay down likelihoods and forms of hope.
> L. BARDOLPH. Yes, if this present quality of war,
> Indeed the instant action, a cause on foot,
> Lives so in hope, as in an early spring
> We see the appearing buds; which to prove fruit,
> Hope gives not so much warrant as despair
> That frosts will bite them. [6]

This is followed by an elaboration of the parable of the man who began to build and, because he had not counted the cost, was not able to finish (*Luke*, xiv, 28-30):

> Like one that draws the model of a house
> Beyond his power to build it; who, half through,
> Gives o'er and leaves his part-created cost
> A naked subject to the weeping clouds,
> And waste for churlish winter's tyranny.

The Archbishop of York then intervenes on the side of immediate action—

> The commonwealth is sick of their own choice;
> Their over-greedy love hath surfeited:
> An habitation giddy and unsure
> Hath he that buildeth on the vulgar heart . . . ,

and it is characteristic of this play that the very fickleness of the common people, dwelt on at some length, should be used to point an obvious moral—'What trust is in these times?'—and, simultaneously, adduced as a ground for optimism. It is the impetuous Hastings who carries his policy and, with unintended irony, hustles off his fellows to try their chance:

> We are time's subjects, and time bids be gone.

The world of *King Henry IV, Part II*—the world we
are introduced to in the first Act—is a world where men
are only too plainly time's subjects, yet persist in planning
and contriving and attempting by hook or by crook to
further their own interests. Most of them, drawing a
model of a desirable future beyond their power to build,
are, in the course of the play, disappointed. Since there is
no close poetic texture lengthy quotation is unnecessary,
but it is worth remarking how often the pattern of hope
and disappointment is repeated. Hotspur at Shrewsbury
—so we are reminded early in the play—had 'lined himself with hope',

> Eating the air on promise of supply,
> Flattering himself in project of a power
> Much smaller than the smallest of his thoughts.
> And so, with great imagination
> Proper to madmen, led his powers to death,
> And winking leap'd into destruction.
>
> (I. iii. 27-33)

The news of Hotspur's death reaches Northumberland
hard on the heels of 'certain news' ('As good as heart can
wish') of rebel victory. In the very scene in which
Hotspur's folly is recalled the rebel leaders allow themselves an over-optimistic estimate of their resources, as we
see when, before the encounter with the royal forces,
Northumberland again defaults, sending 'hearty prayers'
for their success instead of men: 'Thus do the hopes we
have in him touch ground' (IV. i. 17). When the king's
generals offer to negotiate, Hastings (who might indeed
adopt Pistol's somewhat travel-stained motto, 'Si fortune
me tormente, sperato me contento') finds fresh grounds
for optimism: 'Our peace shall stand as firm as rocky
mountains' (IV. i. 188)—and on that note the rebel
generals walk into the prepared trap. It may of course be
said that a play about an unsuccessful rebellion was bound

55

to put some emphasis on frustrated hopes; but it is not only the Northumberland faction who provide examples of the ironic discrepancy between what is planned for and what is achieved. Henry Bolingbroke, caught in the toils of 'necessity' (for 'to end one doubt by death Revives two greater in the heirs of life' (IV. i. 199-200)), spends his powers seeking an elusive stability. It is when this is almost achieved, the long-planned crusade about to be embarked on—'And every thing lies level to our wish' (IV. iv. 7)—that his own strength fails him. The scene in which he hears of the rebel overthrow is indeed an obvious parallel to that in which Northumberland declared that ill tidings 'have in some measure made me well' (I. i. 139):

> And wherefore should these good news make me sick?
> Will Fortune never come with both hands full,
> But write her fair words still in foulest letters? . . .
> I should rejoice now at this happy news;
> And now my sight fails, and my brain is giddy . . .
>
> (IV. iv. 103-9)

It is of course true that Henry has the satisfaction of a reconciliation with his eldest son, and dies hoping that the reign of Henry V will be quieter than his own,

> for what in me was purchased,
> Falls upon thee in a more fairer sort.

But in the imaginative impact of the play as a whole Hal's robust assertion of *de facto* sovereignty

> —My gracious liege,
> You won it [the crown], wore it, kept it, gave it me;
> Then plain and right must my possession be—

counts for little beside the bleak and disillusioned summary of his reign that the elder Henry has just given his son (IV. v. 183 ff.). As for Falstaff, there is the superb comedy of the scene where he and his companions indulge themselves in what, to any sober view, is the most imbecile bit of wishful thinking that ever deluded poor mortals.

PISTOL. Sir John, thy tender lambkin now is king; Harry the fifth's the man . . .
FALSTAFF. What, is the old king dead?
PISTOL. As nail in door: the things I speak are just.
FALSTAFF. Away, Bardolph! saddle my horse. Master Robert Shallow, choose what office thou wilt in the land, 'tis thine. Pistol! I will double-charge thee with dignities.
BARDOLPH. O joyful day!
I would not take a knighthood for my fortune.
PISTOL. What! I do bring good news.
FALSTAFF. Carry Master Silence to bed. Master Shallow, my Lord Shallow,—be what thou wilt; I am fortunes steward—get on thy boots: we'll ride all night. O sweet Pistol! Away Bardolph! [*Exit* BARDOLPH] Come, Pistol, utter more to me; and withal devise something to do thyself good. Boot, boot, Master Shallow! I know the young king is sick for me. Let us take any man's horses; the laws of England are at my commandmont. Blessed are they that have been my friends; and woe to my lord chief justice!
PISTOL. Let vultures vile seize on his lungs also!
'Where is the life that late I led?' say they:
Why, here it is; welcome these pleasant days!

In this context it is plain that the King's mutability speech already quoted (p. 52, above) is not just a bit of moralizing appropriate to a sick and disappointed man. It is not merely 'in character'; it is an explicit formulation of feelings and attitudes deeply embedded in the play. Act III, the central act, has only two scenes, one at court, one in Gloucestershire, and the second succeeds the first without a break. With the King's words still in our ears we are given (among other things) one of the most superb variations in English literature on the theme of *le temps perdu*. Act III, scene ii, like the later Cotswold scenes, is firmly rooted in the actual. Life is going on in this little bit of rural England, and will go on, for all the wars and civil wars now and to come—the smith must be paid, the hade land sown with red wheat, and the well-chain mended[7]. That life is vividly present to us, built up little by little with unobtrusive art. But the scene is drenched in memory. In the first fifty lines, as Shallow recalls the poor pranks of his mad days at Clement's Inn, the exploits of young Jack Falstaff who is now old, and of old Double who is dead, we are at least as much aware of the past (and of the fact that it *is* the past) as of anything in the present. There follows the arrival of Bardolph and Falstaff and the play with the conscripts: Mouldy, whose old mother has no one else to do 'her husbandry and her drudgery', the thin Shadow, the ragged Wart, Feeble the woman's taylor, who has a stout heart and—like Hamlet —a philosophic mind[8], Bullcalf who has a cough 'caught with ringing in the king's affairs upon his coronation-day'—all of them, though two escape the press, 'mortal men' who 'owe God a death'. Then the theme of times past—part memory, part make-believe—is taken up again. 'Doth she hold her own well?' Shallow asks Falstaff of Jane Nightwork.

FALSTAFF. Old, old, Master Shallow.
SHALLOW. Nay, she must be old; she cannot choose but be old; certain she's old; and had Robin Nightwork by old Nightwork before I came to Clement's Inn.
SILENCE. That's fifty years ago.
SHALLOW. Ha, cousin Silence, that thou hadst seen that that this knight and I have seen! Ha, Sir John, said I well?
FALSTAFF. We have heard the chimes at midnight, Master Shallow.

SHALLOW. That we have, that we have, that we have; in faith, Sir John, we have: our watch-word was 'Hem boys!' Come, let's to dinner; come, let's to dinner: Jesus, the days that we have seen! Come, come.   (III. ii. 200-15)

3

Now there are obvious ways in which the dominant mood of the play can be related to the mood of so many of the Sonnets; for here before us we

> perceive that men as plants increase,
> Cheered and check'd even by the self-same sky,
> Vaunt in their youthful sap, at height decrease,
> And wear their brave state out of memory.

2 *Henry IV*, like the Sonnets, is permeated by 'the conceit of this inconstant stay', and for an understanding of the play itself, as for any attempt to understand the Shakespearean progress, it is necessary to see how the constant sense of time—of time as mere sequence, bringing change—shapes the matter before us. Yet to put the matter thus, necessary as it is, is to give a partial and one-sided impression. Unqualified, the account so far given falsifies the imaginative impact of a play that is more lively, more complex, and more far-reaching in its implications than I have so far been able to suggest.

The tone of the play is sombre; but it could not possibly be called pessimistic or depressed. Not only is there the vigour of mind with which the political theme is grasped and presented, there is, in the Falstaff scenes, a familiar comic verve together with an outgoing sympathy—even, at times, liking—for what is so firmly judged. It is important, here, to say neither more nor less than one means, and humour is of all literary qualities the most difficult to handle. Where, as in Shakespeare or Jonson or Molière, humour serves a serious, a truly imaginative purpose, the commentator who tries to define the purpose is likely to cut an odd figure in the eyes of those whose gusto prefers to dwell exclusively on the fun. And indeed there is something comic in a pedagogic or literary-critical handling of things that make you laugh. In *King Henry IV, Part II*, there is nothing, to my taste, so funny as the scene of the mock-kings in *Part I*; but there is the superb incoherence of Mrs Quickly, there is Pistol's constant re-creation of the dramatic part in which he lives[9], there is the exquisite absence of positive presence in Silence; and Falstaff, though he can sometimes go through the motions of wit without the reality (a failure that seems, on Shakespeare's part, deliberate) can still sometimes surprise us with the sheer agility of his self-defence. These things are there, and we can only suppose that the mind that created them enjoyed them. But in relation to our larger themes the significance for us is this: we know that we are dealing with a free mind—one that is neither driven by, nor bent on driving, an 'idea'; the sombre preoccupations are not obsessions.

And Shakespeare shows a further characteristic of great genius: he can feel for, can even invest with dignity, those representative human types who, in the complex play of attitudes that constitute his dramatic statement, are judged and found wanting. When Falstaff celebrates with Doll Tearsheet, at the Boar's Head Tavern, his departure for the wars (II. iv), there is nothing comic in the exhibition of senile lechery. Yet the tipsy Doll can move us with, 'Come, I'll be friends with thee, Jack: thou art going to the wars; and whether I shall ever see thee again or no, there is nobody cares'. And at the end of the scene Mrs Quickly too has her moment, when sentimentality itself is transformed simply by looking towards those human decencies and affections for which—the realities being absent—it must do duty:

Well, fare thee well: I have known thee these twenty
nine years, come peascod time; but an honester and
truer-hearted man,—well, fare thee well.

There is nothing facile in Shakespeare's charity; it is
simply that Shakespeare, like Chaucer, is not afraid of his
spontaneous feelings, and his feelings are not—so to speak
—afraid of each other.

Here, then, is one way in which the insistent elegiac
note is both qualified and deepened. There is yet another.
We have already noticed the repeated references to
Falstaff's age and diseases. But it is not only Falstaff who
is diseased. Northumberland is sick, or 'crafty-sick'; the
King is dying; and the imagery of disease links the individuals to the general action.

> Then you perceive the body of our kingdom
> How foul it is; what rank diseases grow,
> And with what danger, near the heart of it.
>
> (III. i. 38-40)

The King speaks here the same language as the Archbishop
who opposes him:

> . . . we are all diseased,
> And with our surfeiting and wanton hours
> Have brought ourselves into a burning fever,
> And we must bleed for it.
>
> (IV. i. 54-7)

Now disease is not simply, like old age, an inevitable
result of time. Disease, in this play as in others, is associated with disorder originating in the will. The land is
sick because of an original act of usurpation, and because
of the further self-seeking of those who helped Bolingbroke to the throne, and because people like Falstaff think
that 'the law of nature' [10] is different from and can over-
ride the law of justice.

In the light of this we can understand why the feelings
associated with time in this play are not simply feelings of

61

pathos ('And is old Double dead?'). As Mr Traversi has remarked in an excellent essay[11], 'allied to the idea of Time in this play is the conception of over-ruling necessity. . . . *Necessity* is a fact generally accepted by all the political characters . . . All are "time's subjects" '. Now it is certainly true that we are very much aware of time's power; all the strivings of the characters are shadowed by it. But the word 'time' (or 'times'), so frequently appearing, more often than not means the present age, the present state of affairs; and it is with 'the times' in this sense that, again and again, there is associated the compulsion or 'necessity' invoked by both sides in the political quarrel:

We see which way the stream of time doth run,
And are enforced from our most quiet shore
By the rough torrent of occasion.

The time misorder'd doth, in common sense,
Crowd us and crush us to this monstrous form,
To hold our safety up. [12]

'Time's subjects', in short, are men compelled because they are followers of that policy, or self-interest, which works, and can only work, 'on leases of short-number'd hours'[13]. And it is because they accept the times—the world's standards, the shifting pattern of warring interests —that they are ruled by Time, that it is impossible for them to see the temporal process as other than absolute: 'Let time shape, and there an end'.

I hope this does not seem like putting Shakespeare on the rack of a demand for a moral at any price. Shakespeare never explicitly points a moral; and it will be some years before he fully reveals in terms of the awakened imagination why those that follow their noses are led by their eyes, or what it really means to be the fool of time. For the moment we are only concerned with the direction that

his developing insight is taking; and it seems to me that
what is coming into consciousness is nothing less than an
awareness of how men make the world that they inhabit,
an understanding of the relation between what men are
and the kind of perceptions they have about the nature
of things. It is this growing awareness, linking the overt
social criticism with the more deep-lying and pervasive
concern with time's power, that explains our sense of
fundamental issues coming to expression. It explains why
the tone of 2 *Henry IV* is entirely different from the tone
of detached observation of the earlier plays. In Act I,
scene i, Northumberland, finding physic in the poison of
ill news, throws away his crutch and 'sickly quoif'.

> Now bind my brows with iron; and approach
> The ragged'st hour that time and spite dare bring
> To frown upon the enraged Northumberland!
> Let heaven kiss earth! now let not Nature's hand
> Keep the wild flood confined! let order die!
> And let this world no longer be a stage
> To feed contention in a lingering act;
> But let one spirit of the first-born Cain
> Reign in all bosoms, that, each heart being set
> On bloody courses, the rude scene may end,
> And darkness be the burier of the dead!

These lines, placed as they are at the climax of the first
scene of the play, are intended to be taken with deadly
seriousness: this is what is implied in Northumberland's
'aptest way for safety and revenge'. If the note of horror
seems momentarily to go beyond the prevailing mood of
the play (it is a note more appropriate to *Lear* or
Macbeth[14]), it is not discordant with that mood which,
even without this vision of anarchy, is sombre enough.

Henry IV, *Part II*, is markedly a transitional play. It
looks back to the Sonnets and the earlier history plays,
and it looks forward to the great tragedies. In technique

too we are beginning to find that more complete permeation of the material by the shaping imagination which distinguishes the plays that follow it from those that went before[15]. The words do not yet strike to unsuspected depths (it is significant that some of the most vividly realized scenes are in prose); but in the manner of its working the play is nearer to *Macbeth* than to *Richard III*; the imagery is organic to the whole, and the verse and prose alike are beginning to promote that associative activity that I have tried to define as the distinguishing mark of great poetic drama. It is this imaginative wholeness that allows us to say that Shakespeare is now wholly *within* his material. As a result the play has that doubleness which, as T. S. Eliot says, is a characteristic of the greatest poetry[16], and the more obvious qualities of action, satire, humour and pathos are informed and integrated by a serious vision of life subjected to time.

CHAPTER IV

The Theme of Appearance and Reality in
Troilus and Cressida

AT the period when Shakespeare wrote the Second Part of *King Henry IV* his concern with the domination of life by time was not an exclusive preoccupation. It did not prevent him from getting on with the business of living or from writing plays that had nothing to do with time's thievish progress to eternity. Neither was it a philosophical interest in an abstract problem. It was simply a part of his imaginative apprehension of life; and since its expression coincided with a remarkable development of his dramatic power we might presume—even without the evidence of the Sonnets—that it had for him a special significance.

Now a deeply ingrained preoccupation with time almost inevitably brings with it two further allied preoccupations—with death and with appearance and reality. With death, because it is the supreme instance of the disturbing and thwarting aspects of time's action. With appearance and reality because the mere passage of time

—whose million'd accidents
Creep in 'twixt vows, and change decrees of kings—

reveals different aspects of the world we thought we knew[1]. These new aspects may contradict, or seem to contradict, the impressions to which, assuming them to represent an unchangeable reality, we have committed ourselves; and as a consequence an honest and energetic spirit is forced to ask himself what is solid and enduring in the flux.

There is always the risk of anticipating and imposing where it is our business to discover. But there is no doubt that during the period immediately preceding the great tragedies preoccupations such as these entered deeply into Shakespeare's dramatic poetry. I have already remarked that Shakespeare does not deal with his themes in the manner of one embarking on a dispassionate enquiry into the sources of self-deceit and the domination of men by appearances. All we can say is that the way experience came to him was soaked in feelings and shot through with perceptions that crystallized out as the themes of appearance, death, and so on. But the condition of the defining that his art *is*, was that it should remain as close as possible to the level of presented experience; for the defining is, simultaneously, an exploring. Our talk of themes, in consequence, is simply a way of pointing to the centres of consciousness that exert a kind of gravitational pull, to the dominant tones and emphases of a living mode of experience. Moreover, to use phrases suggesting that Shakespeare is simply an analyst of experience is to obscure the urgent personal nature of the imaginative effort and its genuinely exploratory nature. Thus we may for convenience speak of Shakespeare's investigation of the world of appearance and the power of illusion; but this is not an investigation proceeding from established positions to logical conclusions. Indeed in *Troilus and Cressida*, of which I now wish to speak, there are no conclusions[2].

I

I have said that Shakespeare's way of presenting and defining is not 'philosophical'. But *Troilus and Cressida*, though far from abstract, comes nearer than any other of the plays to being a philosophical debate. Greeks and Trojans represent different values, and the things they stand for are the subject of frequent exposition, debate and explicit comment[3]. We shall not do violence to the play or wrench its total meaning if we hinge our analysis on three of the major sequences in which there is a deliberate presentation or development of 'ideas' embodied in the action. On certain conditions: first, that we retain a lively sense of the dramatic context of each formal exposition, with its attendant ironies; secondly that we observe in each instance where the poetry qualifies, and where it enters into and reinforces, whatever may be offered by way of statement. There is a third condition, or qualification, which will be mentioned in due course.

We may begin with Ulysses' famous speech in the first meeting of the Greek generals (I. iii).

> Troy, yet upon his basis, had been down,
> And the great Hector's sword had lack'd a master,
> But for these instances.
> The specialty of rule has been neglected:
> And, look, how many Grecian tents do stand
> Hollow upon this plain, so many hollow factions.
> When that the general is not like the hive
> To whom the foragers shall all repair,
> What honey is expected? Degree being vizarded,
> The unworthiest shows as fairly in the mask.
> The heavens themselves, the planets, and this
>   centre,
> Observe degree, priority, and place,
> Insisture, course, proportion, season, form,
> Office, and custom, in all line of order:
> And therefore is the glorious planet Sol
> In noble eminence enthron'd and spher'd
> Amidst the other; whose med'cinable eye
> Corrects the ill aspects of planets evil,
> And posts, like the commandment of a king,
> Sans check to good and bad: but when the planets
> In evil mixture to disorder wander,

What plagues, and what portents, what mutiny,
What raging of the sea, shaking of earth,
Commotion in the winds, frights, changes, horrors,
Divert and crack, rend and deracinate
The unity and married calm of states
Quite from their fixture! O, when degree is shak'd,
Which is the ladder to all high designs,
The enterprise is sick! How could communities,
Degrees in schools, and brotherhoods in cities,
Peaceful commerce from dividable shores,
The primogenity and due of birth,
Prerogative of age, crowns, sceptres, laurels,
But by degree, stand in authentic place?
Take but degree away, untune that string,
And, hark! what discord follows; each thing meets
In mere oppugnancy: the bounded waters
Should lift their bosoms higher than the shores,
And make a sop of all this solid globe:
Strength should be lord of imbecility,
And the rude son should strike his father dead:
Force should be right; or rather, right and wrong,
Between whose endless jar justice resides,
Should lose their names, and so should justice too.
Then every thing includes itself in power,
Power into will, will into appetite;
And appetite, an universal wolf,
So doubly seconded with will and power,
Must make perforce an universal prey,
And last eat up himself. Great Agamemnon,
This chaos, when degree is suffocate,
Follows the choking.

Commentators have perhaps been too much impressed by
this piece of rhetoric. One speaks for oneself, but to my
mind the only part that by Shakespearean standards is
great poetry is the last—'Then everything includes itself
in power . . .' For the rest (in spite of some striking lines),
the expansive insistence, the smooth unimpeded rhythms,

and the general tone of a public address, denote a formal
declamation on one of the great Elizabethan commonplaces. I cannot feel, in short, that Shakespeare is *behind*
this speech until his imagination catches fire at the vision
of the 'chaos' consequent on the unchecked exercise of
'appetite'. The speech, it is true, is one to keep hold of in
reading the play as representing, in its way, a positive. It
is at least equally important to observe that none of the
Greek generals in any significant sense embodies the order
that is talked about; none has the right to represent the
integration for which Ulysses pleads. It is not merely that
Achilles, disordered in himself, breaks the unity of the
Greek camp,—'Kingdom'd Achilles in commotion rages
And batters down himself' (II. iii. 184-5); whatever the
claims that the Greek generals may make for themselves[4] the impression we get from their counsels is one
of 'policy' rather than of 'wisdom'. To engineer Achilles
back into position as 'the sinew and the forehand of our
host' they descend to a stratagem that, in the working
out, is not a very impressive piece of statecraft. Ajax is to
be set up against Achilles and the latter appealed to by his
ignoble pride.

> Two curs shall tame each other: pride alone
> Must tarre the mastiffs on, as 'twere their bone.
>
> (I. iii. 390-1)

It is Nestor, not Thersites, who speaks these lines.

The scene in which Ulysses carries out this characteristic
bit of diplomacy gives us the second of the sequences that
deserve some special attention. Ajax is flattered, and
Achilles deliberately slighted. To him, thus worked on,
Ulysses enters reading.

ACHILLES.   Here is Ulysses:
    I'll interrupt his reading.
    How now, Ulysses!

ULYSSES.   Now, great Thetis' son!
ACHILLES. What are you reading?
ULYSSES.   A strange fellow here
Writes me: That man, how dearly ever parted,
How much in having, or without, or in,
Cannot make boast to have that which he hath,
Nor feels not what he owes but by reflection;
As when his virtues shining upon others
Heat them, and they retort that heat again
To the first giver.
ACHILLES.   This is not strange, Ulysses.
The beauty that is borne here in the face
The bearer knows not, but commends itself
To others' eyes: nor doth the eye itself,
That most pure spirit of sense, behold itself,
Not going from itself; but eye to eye oppos'd
Salutes each other with each other's form;
For speculation turns not to itself
Till it hath travell'd, and is married there
Where it may see itself. This is not strange at all.
                                    (III. iii. 94-111)

It has been pointed out[5] that the 'strange fellow' is
Plato, and that in these lines there is an echo of the *First
Alcibiades* (132, 133). Socrates, urging that the soul only
comes to know itself by contemplating soul and 'things
divine', uses the analogy of the eye. (In Jowett's trans-
lation, 'If the eye is to see itself, it must look at the eye,
and at that part of the eye where sight which is the virtue
of the eye resides'.) Now in the Dialogue (which may or
may not be Plato's) the analogy is part of an argument
that leads up to the necessity for the statesman of self-
knowledge. That Achilles uses the Platonic image to
express an admirable sense of the need for mutuality and
creative interplay is not a violent wrenching of the original
analogy. What is significant is the further twist given

70

to the argument by Ulysses, who is concerned neither with self-knowledge nor with mutual relationships. What he is concerned with—indeed the whole set of assumptions on which his statesmanship is based—is soon apparent. To Achilles' 'This is not strange at all', he replies:

> I do not strain at the position,
> It is familiar, but at the author's drift;
> Who in his circumstance expressly proves
> That no man is the lord of anything,
> Though in and of him there be much consisting,
> Till he communicate his parts to others:
> Nor doth he of himself know them for aught
> Till he behold them form'd in the applause
> Where they're extended; who, like an arch, reverberates
> The voice again, or, like a gate of steel
> Fronting the sun, receives and renders back
> His figure and his heat.

(III. iii. 112-23)

The snake in the grass comes out at 'applause'. And in the hard metallic imagery that follows there is nothing at all corresponding to the Socratic argument, nor is there anything of the organic suggestion of Achilles' 'marriage' metaphor. Neither the arch nor the gate of steel can convey any suggestion of creative mutuality. But the implications of these similes are best seen when we have followed the exchange to its end.

There is now a further twist in Ulysses' argument. Man, he has asserted, only knows his true worth in society: he needs society because it gives him honour and applause. But worth, he proceeds to suggest, isn't really necessary to obtain the public 'reverberation'. Society can create an appearance of worth even when there is no substantial basis for it.

71

I was much rapt in this;
And apprehended here immediately
The unknown Ajax.
Heavens, what a man is there! a very horse;
That has he knows not what. Nature, what things
    there are
Most abject in regard, and dear in use!
What things, again most dear in the esteem,
And poor in worth! Now shall we see tomorrow,—
An act that very chance doth throw upon him,—
Ajax renown'd . . .
To see these Grecian lords! why, even already
They clap the lubber Ajax on the shoulder . . .
                                        (III. iii. 123-39)

That the Greeks do not in fact esteem the lubber Ajax,
that Ulysses despises Achilles' craving for applause[6], and
that the whole speech is part of a deliberate stratagem,
these facts do not affect the underlying significance of
what is said. Ulysses thinks throughout in terms of a
public world, in which men are manipulated and it is the
public appearance that counts.

And now occurs one of the most interesting transitions
in the play. To Achilles' exclamation, 'What! are my
deeds forgot?' Ulysses replies with a vivid and vigorous
passage on the inevitable connexion between time and
oblivion.

Time hath, my lord, a wallet at his back,
Wherein he puts alms for oblivion,
A great-sized monster of ingratitudes:
Those scraps are good deeds past; which are devour'd
As fast as they are made, forgot as soon
As done: perseverance, dear my lord,
Keeps honour bright: to have done is to hang
Quite out of fashion, like a rusty mail
In monumental mockery. Take the instant way;
For honours travel in a strait so narrow

72

Where one but goes abreast: keep then the path;
For emulation hath a thousand sons
That one by one pursue: if you give way,
Or hedge aside from the direct forthright,
Like to an enter'd tide they all rush by
And leave you hindmost;
Or, like a gallant horse fall'n in first rank,
Lie there for pavement to the abject rear,
O'errun and trampled on: then what they do in
    present,
Though less than yours in past, must o'ertop yours;
For time is like a fashionable host,
That slightly shakes his parting guest by the hand,
And with his arms outstretch'd, as he would fly,
Grasps in the comer: welcome ever smiles,
And farewell goes out sighing. O! let not virtue seek
Remuneration for the thing it was;
For beauty, wit,
High birth, vigour of bone, desert in service,
Love, friendship, charity, are subjects all
To envious and calumniating time.
One touch of nature makes the whole world kin,
That all with one consent praise new-born gauds,
Though they are made and moulded of things past,
And give to dust that is a little gilt
More laud than gilt o'er-dusted.
The present eye praises the present object:
Then marvel not, thou great and complete man,
That all the Greeks begin to worship Ajax;
Since things in motion sooner catch the eye
Than what not stirs. The cry went once on thee,
And still it might, and yet it may again,
If thou would'st not entomb thyself alive,
And case thy reputation in thy tent;
Whose glorious deeds, but in these fields of late,
Made emulous missions 'mongst the gods themselves,
And drave great Mars to faction.

(III. iii. 145-90)

73

Neither the poetic force of this, nor the fact that it echoes the Sonnets, should lead us to take it, unqualified, as a direct expression of Shakespeare's 'philosophy'. There is an urgency that comes from feelings deeply stirred; and at one point there is what sounds like a note of personal bitterness—

> For beauty, wit,
> High birth, vigour of bone, desert in service,
> Love, friendship, charity, are subjects all
> To envious and calumniating time.

But it is still Ulysses who is speaking, and Ulysses is still predominantly concerned not with the effect of time on man's life in general but with the relation between time and reputation. Love, friendship and charity are strange intruders from beyond the public world, where what counts is honour, praise and remuneration[7]. It is all perfectly in keeping. Committed to appearances you are inevitably committed to time. Accept time as the governing reality and you can only see 'good deeds' as 'scraps' devoured by oblivion. All that remains is the anxiety-ridden struggle (expressed in the repeated imagery of physical effort, 'keep then the path' and so on) to keep up with the fleeting present. These are the logical consequences of the assumptions that underlie the philosophy of the Greeks. For all their formal dignity they are creatures of time and appearance[8].

2

Shakespeare's Greeks stand for public life and an impersonal 'reason', divorced from feeling and intuitive intelligence. The Trojans are their complementary opposite. Corresponding to the meeting of the Greek generals in the first act is the Trojan council in the second. The question is whether or not Helen shall be retained and the war continued. Of the two leading speakers, Hector appeals to reason and morality, the law of nature and the law of nations, all of which decree that Helen shall be sent back to her husband. He is, significantly, overborne by Troilus, whose idiomatic vigour of speech ('you fur your gloves with reasons') proclaims an intensely personal approach to matters that Hector tries to see as examples of a general law. Troilus's theme, like that of Ulysses to Achilles later, is 'honour'—and honour means standing up for your own valuations, for 'What is aught but as 'tis valued?' (II. ii. 52). Troilus is an excellent orator. What could be more reasonable than the tone and manner of the lines in which he counters Hector's objections?

> I take to-day a wife, and my election
> Is led on in the conduct of my will;
> My will enkindled by mine eyes and ears,
> Two traded pilots 'twixt the dangerous shores
> Of will and judgment. How may I avoid,
> Although my will distaste what it elected,
> The wife I chose? there can be no evasion
> To blench from this and to stand firm by honour . . .
>
> (II. ii. 61-8)

Yet what could be more absurd than to speak of the senses as mediating between the judgment and the will? It is the judgment that is the pilot or mediator between the senses and the will. Since Troilus has in fact abjured reason—'Nay, if we talk of reason, let's shut our gates and sleep' (II. ii. 46-7)—we need not waste time trying to find a moral or psychological system that will make sense of the 'traded pilots' and the 'dangerous shores'[9]. The talk of 'judgment' is bluff,—though it sounds like unconscious bluff. What matters is 'will', and what the will has once 'elected' 'honour' demands that it shall stand by. The scene has a livelier dramatic interest than can appear from quotation or summary. But what is significant for us in the present connexion is that Troilus embodies a

mode of judgment based entirely on the subjective
ground of passion and will. Hector is there to provide the
apt comment,—

> The reasons you allege do more conduce
> To the hot passion of distemper'd blood
> Than to make up a free determination
> 'Twixt right and wrong.
>
> (II. ii. 168-71)

But it is Troilus who wins the day.

There is the same intense subjectivism in Troilus's love
poetry.

> I am giddy, expectation whirls me round.
> The imaginary relish is so sweet
> That it enchants my sense. What will it be
> When that the watery palate tastes indeed
> Love's thrice repured nectar? death, I fear me,
> Sounding destruction, or some joy too fine,
> Too subtle-potent, tun'd too sharp in sweetness
> For the capacity of my ruder powers:
> I fear it much; and I do fear besides
> That I shall lose distinction in my joys;
> As doth a battle, when they charge on heaps
> The enemy flying.
>
> (III. ii. 17-28)

It would be difficult to improve on what Mr Traversi
has said about this and allied passages. There is, he says, 'a
poignant thinness' in the love imagery, which conveys
simultaneously 'an impression of intense feeling and an
underlying lack of content'. Of the passage just quoted he
says, 'The emotions . . . are intense enough, but only in
the palate and the senses; they scarcely involve any full
personality in the speaker'. And he further points out that
the expression of Troilus's 'idealism' through the imagery
of taste underlines its unsubstantiality and its subjection
to time. It is, we may say, the over-active element of

subjective fantasy in Troilus's passion that gives to his love poetry its hurried, fevered note, with a suggestion of trying to realize something essentially unrealizable. The actual separation of the lovers, so far from being a turning-point, is in a sense merely incidental, for it only emphasizes what is in fact intrinsic to their relationship. The poetry of parting strikes a note almost identical with the poetry of anticipation.

> Injurious time now with a robber's haste
> Crams his rich thievery up, he knows not how:
> As many farewells as be stars in heaven,
> With distinct breath and consign'd kisses to them,
> He fumbles up into a loose adieu,
> And scants us with a single famish'd kiss,
> Distasted with the salt of broken tears.[10]
>
> (IV. iv. 42-7)

It is here that I find myself most in disagreement with Professor Wilson Knight. Professor Knight makes some necessary distinctions (he was I believe the first to do so) between Greek intellect and Trojan intuition; but he seems to me to attribute to the latter a more positive value than did Shakespeare. It is not merely that Time slays Troilus's love—'a spiritual and delicate thing'—the whole basis of that love and of the 'idealism' of which it is a part is subjected to as radical a criticism as is the Greek 'reason'. It is Troilus's subjectivism that commits him to a world of time, appearance, and what M. Fluchère calls 'an intolerable anxiety'. It is, in short, not opposed but complementary to the public realism of the Greeks.

3

I have spoken of a further condition that must qualify our approach to the play through an analysis of the more direct presentation of its major themes in the crucial passages that we have examined. It is difficult to say exactly how we experience the play, not as a succession of parts but as a living whole. But when we experience it directly in this way it is plain that what we have to deal with, what we are engaged in, is not simply an objective analysis of the ways in which apparently opposed attitudes lead to the same predicament. *Troilus and Cressida,* says M. Fluchère, 'is a play with many facets, and recent critics have quite rightly underlined its ambiguity. Over the two great themes of Love and War situations develop which are the most likely to confuse the reader's mind'. In other words, we—the spectators—are directly involved; and it is our confusion that largely contributes to the ambiguousness intrinsic to the play. The material that Shakespeare chose to work on was public property. His audience, he knew, would have some preconceived notions about Agamemnon, Ulysses, Helen and the rest. And he weaves these preconceptions into the texture of the play by the simple device of now appearing to endorse them, now turning them upside down. We are rarely quite clear about the judgment we are required to make. In the Greek camp we may imagine for a time that we have in fact before us the wise and dignified figures of legend. But it is not only Thersites who undermines that notion: the generals are quite capable of doing it for themselves; and quite early in the play we find ourselves echoing the words of Aeneas,—

> How may
> A stranger to those most imperial looks
> Know them from eyes of other mortals?
>
> (I. iii. 222-4)

Helen, we are reminded by Troilus, is

> a Grecian queen, whose youth and freshness
> Wrinkles Apollo's, and makes stale the morning
>
> (II. ii. 78-9)

—the figure of legend; but to say that she 'turn'd crown'd

78

kings to merchants' (II. ii. 83) is not unambiguous praise; and the Helen of the play seems quite at home in the atmosphere of silly smart-talk that Pandarus reports (uncritically and at length) to Cressida (I. ii). As for Cressida, she exists mainly in the imagination of Troilus. So far as she is presented directly, she is the wanton of tradition and is made deliberately to refer to her traditional role (III. ii. 195 ff.), as Pandarus immediately afterwards does to his. Yet there is, surely, the note of sincerity in her response to Troilus's declaration of love—'Prince Troilus, I have loved you night and day For many weary months' (III. ii. 124-5). The ambiguity that we are made to feel— and not merely to analyse—springs from the shifting appearances of the characters as well as from the trickiness and dubiety of the formal exposition and argument. We, the spectators, in short, are involved in the play's confusions.

We are thus prepared for the way in which Troilus's speech at the play's climax strikes home.

> This she? no; this is Diomed's Cressida.
> If beauty have a soul, this is not she;
> If souls guide vows, if vows be sanctimonies,
> If sanctimony be the gods' delight,
> If there be rule in unity itself,
> This is not she. O madness of discourse,
> That cause sets up with and against thyself;
> Bi-fold authority! where reason can revolt
> Without perdition, and loss assume all reason
> Without revolt: this is, and is not, Cressid.
> Within my soul there doth conduce a fight
> Of this strange nature that a thing inseparate
> Divides more wider than the sky and earth;
> And yet the spacious breadth of this division
> Admits no orifice for a point as subtle
> As Ariachne's broken woof to enter.
> Instance, O instance! strong as Pluto's gates;

Cressid is mine, tied with the bonds of heaven:
Instance, O instance! strong as heaven itself;
The bonds of heaven are slipp'd, dissolv'd, and
    loos'd;
And with another knot, five-finger-tied,
The fractions of her faith, orts of her love,
The fragments, scraps, the bits and greasy reliques
Of her o'er-eaten faith, are bound to Diomed.

(v. ii. 133-56)

Dispassionately considered, these lines complete the demonstration of the identity in opposition of the Greeks and Trojans. Troilus's love—which focuses the Trojan 'idealism' as Ulysses' policy makes manifest the latent implications of Greek 'reason'—has been finally shown as subject to time and change. And he now embodies in his own person the disorder envisaged in Ulysses' speech on degree. But it is hardly possible to consider this poetry dispassionately. The powerful varied rhythms, the marked transition from the quasi-logical manner of the opening to the muscular and vividly sensory imagery of the close, the impossibility of reading the lines without sensing behind them the urgency of a whole personality in the toils,—all these make plain how remote this is from the poetry of statement and exposition. The lines pound with an energy that can find no issue, and we ourselves, in the act of grappling with their meaning, experience something analogous to the physical nausea, evoked in the imagery of the concluding lines, that offers the only possible release. This is intended not as rhetoric but as sober description.

O madness of discourse,
That cause sets up with and against thyself;
Bi-fold authority! where reason cán revolt
Without perdition, and loss assume all reason
Without revolt: this is, and is not, Cressid.

It is possible to paraphrase this—though not without attempting to combine alternative readings. But I do not think anyone can make a determined effort to bring to a single focus the various senses of the last two and a half lines without experiencing directly the dizzy bewilderment whose causes they seem simply to describe. We are made directly aware of what is meant by the metaphor of the abysses of the mind. It is not only the personality of Cressida that yawns apart beneath the appearance of identity, just as it is not only, a few lines later, 'the bonds of heaven' that are 'slipp'd, dissolv'd, and loos'd'. It was a deep non-logical apprehension—yet working with a logic of its own—that prompted Shakespeare to run together, in 'Ariachne', the subtle filament of the spider and the clew given to Theseus. We ourselves are in this labyrinth or web. And it is in the labyrinth of appearances that the play leaves us.

That, however, was not where Shakespeare was content to leave himself for long. *Troilus and Cressida* implies more than it contrives to say; and what it implies may be best seen if we consider again the play's position within the Shakespearean sequence.

Time dominates many of the Sonnets; time and death, the Second Part of *King Henry IV*. With that as a kind of premise we may express a central line of development as follows. It cannot have been long after *Henry IV* that Shakespeare wrote *Hamlet*, which is a play about death. The question asked by *Hamlet* (the whole play, not merely the Prince), though obscurely and in a sense inarticulately, concerns an obsession with death. Implicit in the play is a sense of the connexion between an overwhelming consciousness of death and a fear of and recoil from life. *Troilus and Cressida* is more articulate in its

F   81

questioning. Why, Shakespeare seems to be asking, has time its apparently overwhelming power? The answer towards which the play seems to tend is that time is an ultimate reality to those who live in a world of appearance—whether an 'objective' social world, perceived and controlled by the practical reason, a world from which something essential is missing, or a subjective world like Troilus's from which reason is excluded.

Now *Troilus and Cressida* raises a further question, which is simply, How do men come to give themselves to appearances? It is easy enough to see that the 'public' world evoked by Ulysses is a world of appearance, and to sense its limitations. But what of Troilus and his love? Professor Wilson Knight says, 'It is the arch-enemy, Time, that kills values. . . . Throughout this play . . . we have a philosophy of love which regards it as essentially un-at-home in time and incapable of continued concrete embodiment in the difficult flux of events'. Similarly Mr Traversi speaks of 'a flaw inherent in the human situation', of Shakespeare's 'sense of the fatal disharmony introduced by time into the love of Troilus and Cressida'. 'The true tragedy of the play' is 'the sense of the impossibility, the meaninglessness of constancy in a world where time dominates human relationships, and where fulfilment and separation seem inevitable and connected aspects of a single situation'. My own feeling is that the play takes us further than that. The most powerful imaginative effect is of bewilderment, ambiguity, of being in the labyrinth. But we have also seen that implicit in the presentation of Troilus (and Mr Traversi himself brings this out) is a criticism of the kind of attitude and the modes of evaluation that Troilus embodies. Put simply, if something vital is missing from the public world of the Greeks, Troilus's subjectivism is equally flawed. This criticism, a point of genuine new growth, is explicit at one point in the play. In the Trojan council scene we have this:

TROILUS.   What is aught but as 'tis valued?
HECTOR. But value dwells not in particular will;
    It holds his estimate and dignity
    As well wherein 'tis precious of itself
    As in the prizer. 'Tis mad idolatry
    To make the service greater than the god;
    And the will dotes that is inclinable
    To what infectiously itself affects,
    Without some image of the affected merit.
                                        (ii. ii. 52-60)

Here is indicated the direction that any further exploration is forced to take. The lines point directly to *King Lear*, offering us the very terms we have to use in giving ourselves an account of that play. *Lear* opens with an assertion of 'will'. It is a will that 'dotes', so that its possessor is betrayed into rejecting the true good and is delivered to the false appearance. But why does it dote? Because it is 'inclinable to what infectiously itself affects'. What then is 'infection', and what is health? These questions take us to the heart of the human mystery. If *Troilus and Cressida* suggests that subjugation by time and appearance results from false choice and a misdirection of the will, the next step is to bring to consciousness the 'irrational' forces that underlie choice and will. We are forced to ask ourselves nothing less than, What is essential human nature? Still keeping to our patently inadequate formal terms, we may say that it is precisely this question that *King Lear* attempts to answer [11].

CHAPTER V

King Lear

IF, at the end of *King Lear*, we feel that the King's angry and resounding question, 'Who is it that can tell me who I am?' has indeed been answered, that is because Shakespeare has submitted himself to a process equivalent in the emotional and imaginative sphere to the famous Cartesian intellectual doubt. Some of the most funda-mental questions concerning the nature of man are posed in a way that precludes all ready-made answers, that, in fact, so emphasizes the difficulty of the questions as to make any kind of answer seem all but impossible. Only thus could the urgent perplexities of the earlier plays be brought into full consciousness and confronted at the deepest level of significance. For these reasons *King Lear* has the three characteristics of the very greatest works of art: it is timeless and universal; it has a crucial place in its author's inner biography; and it marks a moment of great importance in the changing consciousness of the civiliza-tion to which it belongs. In the preceding chapters I have indicated some of the converging pressures that com-pelled Shakespeare to the writing of *King Lear*. In this chapter I shall be mainly concerned with the play's essential significance as I see it. But before passing from the one to the other, and as a convenient way of bringing to focus this intrinsic significance, I should like briefly to consider the play in its third aspect, as indicating a stage in the emergence of the modern European consciousness. To do this we must first turn from the question of 'human nature' to that of the wider 'Nature' within which human life has its setting. In our own 'philosophies of life', as in

the play, the two questions prove in the long run to be
inseparable.

I

In an essay on 'Nature', published in the posthumous
Three Essays on Religion but written in the eighteen fifties,
John Stuart Mill attempted to clear up some of the con-
fusion that had gathered about that ambiguous word.
The question he was mainly concerned with was whether
Nature, in the sense of that which 'takes place without
the agency, or without the voluntary and intentional
agency, of man', could offer a standard of human conduct.
Should we deliberately, as the phrase goes, 'follow
Nature'? His answer was an emphatic No. Man's progress
is a continual triumph over nature; and although we may
feel awe in the presence of 'the greater natural phenomena
. . . a hurricane; a mountain precipice; the desert; the
ocean, either agitated or at rest; the solar system . . .', we
must not confuse 'the astonishment, rising into awe'
caused by the vastness of these things with the admiration
due to moral excellence, or fondly imagine that their
attributes are such as we ought to emulate.

For how stands the fact? That next to the greatness
of these cosmic forces, the quality which most forcibly
strikes every one who does not avert his eyes from it,
is their perfect and absolute recklessness . . . In sober
truth, nearly all the things which men are hanged or
imprisoned for doing to one another, are nature's
everyday performances. Killing, the most criminal act
recognized by human laws, Nature does once to every
being that lives; and in a large proportion of cases, after
protracted tortures such as only the greatest monsters
whom we read of ever purposely inflicted on their
living fellow-creatures. If, by an arbitrary reservation,
we refuse to account anything murder but what abridges
a certain term supposed to be allotted to human life,

85

Nature also does this to all but a small percentage of lives, and does it in all the modes, violent or insidious, in which the worst human beings take the lives of one another. Nature impales men, breaks them as if on the wheel, casts them to be devoured by wild beasts, burns them to death, crushes them with stones like the first Christian martyrs, starves them with hunger, freezes them with cold, poisons them by the quick or slow venom of her exhalations, and has hundreds of other hideous deaths in reserve, such as the ingenious cruelty of a Nabis or a Domitian never surpassed. All this, Nature does with the most supercilious disregard both of mercy and of justice, emptying her shafts upon the best and noblest indifferently with the meanest and the worst; upon those who are engaged in the highest and worthiest enterprises, and often as the direct consequence of the noblest acts; and it might almost be imagined as a punishment for them. She mows down those on whose existence hangs the well-being of a whole people, perhaps the prospects of the human race for generations to come, with as little compunction as those whose death is a relief to themselves, or a blessing to those under their noxious influence. Such are Nature's dealings with life.

It will be agreed that this passage sounds a familiar nineteenth-century note[1]—and that it could not possibly have been written in the sixteenth century. It certainly was not that the facts that Mill instances— famine, pestilence and so on—were not known, but that no one in the middle ages or in the sixteenth century could have written of Nature in that tone and with those implications. It was taken for granted that Nature was often cruel (there had, after all, been a Fall from Paradise), but the whole disposition of things, independent of man's will, served a providential plan. Nature, in this sense, though subject to disorder, was essentially ordered, and

86

it was ordered for the good of man[2]. George Herbert's poem, 'Providence', shows a world where everything is ordered and all things serve a purpose.

Thy cupboard serves the world: the meat is set,
Where all may reach: no beast but knows his feed.
Birds teach us hawking; fishes have their net:
The great prey on the less, they on some weed.

Nothing ingendred doth prevent his meat:
Flies have their table spread, ere they appeare.
Some creatures have in winter what to eat;
Others do sleep, and envie not their cheer.

How finely dost thou times and seasons spin,
And make a twist checker'd with night and day!
Which as it lengthens windes us in,
As bouls go on, but turning all the way.

Each creature hath a wisdome for his good.
The pigeons feed their tender off-spring, crying,
When they are callow; but withdraw their food
When they are fledge, that need may teach them
flying.

Bees work for man; and yet they never bruise
Their masters flower, but leave it, having done,
As fair as ever, and as fit for use;
So both the flower doth stay, and hony run.

Sheep eat the grasse, and dung the ground for more:
Trees after bearing drop their leaves for soil:
Springs vent their streams, and by expense get store:
Clouds cool by heat, and baths by cooling boil.

We may not always be able to recognize that order, but as Herbert says in the same poem, 'If we could heare Thy skill and art, what musick would it be!'[3]

Within this natural order man had a unique place. There was no question of his 'following Nature' in the vague nineteenth-century sense that was to annoy Mill, but only of realizing the potentialities of his own nature. His nature was corrupted by the Fall, but was capable of receiving Grace. It was 'natural' for him to sin, but his essential nature was fulfilled in doing what he ought to do: so that in another and more important sense 'natural' as applied to man tended to suggest a standard to be achieved,—that which was right and proper for man. Thus Hooker speaks of 'our . . . intent of discovering the natural way, whereby rules have been found out concerning that goodness wherewith the Will of man ought to be moved in human actions; as everything naturally and necessarily doth desire the utmost good and greatest perfection whereof Nature hath made it capable, even so man'[4].

Thus the word 'natural' as applied to man had a peculiar resonance; it was a kind of short-hand that could be used effectively even when the complex philosophical implications were not immediately present. There is a fine passage in Ben Jonson's *The Staple of News* (1626) that illustrates this.

> They covet things
> Superfluous still, when it were much more honour
> They could want necessary: what need hath nature
> Of silver dishes, or gold chamber-pots?
> Of perfumed napkins, or a numerous family
> To see her eat? poor, and wise, she requires
> Meat only; hunger is not ambitious:
> Say, that you were the emperor of pleasures,
> The great dictator of fashions, for all Europe,
> And had the pomp of all the courts, and kingdoms,
> Laid forth unto the shew, to make yourself
> Gazed and admired at; you must go to bed,
> And take your natural rest: then all this vanisheth.

Your bravery was but shown; 'twas not possest:
While it did boast itself, it was then perishing.

(III. ii)

Here, and in similar passages, 'nature' has partly a biological reference: it means what is necessary to maintain
man's natural constitution; and at the same time it refers
to what is customary and sanctioned by tradition in a
certain kind of community. But behind it—adding depth
and volume—is the structure of theological and philosophical belief to which I have referred[5].

A firm conviction of what is distinctively 'natural' or
proper for man does not of course necessarily depend on a
belief in the providential ordering of non-human Nature,
just as relativism in morals does not necessarily follow
from a belief in Nature's indifference, as Mill's essay shows.
But in the age of Shakespeare the partial erosion of the
established assumptions about Nature does seem to have
had a share in the undermining of the older conception of
human nature and the traditional sanctions of morality[6].
By the beginning of the seventeenth century to some
minds Nature was ceasing to appear as a divinely ordained
order and was beginning to appear as an amoral collection
of forces. Now if man himself is *only* part of Nature as
thus conceived, then 'natural impulse' (or so it may be
argued) cannot be questioned; and natural impulse inevitably means the more powerful drives—sexual appetite, the
desire for dominance, and so on. In *Les Libertins en France
au XVIIe Siècle*: F. T. Perrens tells us that the most serious
charge brought by the Jesuit Father Garassus against the
free-thinkers was that they 'recognize no other sovereign
power but Nature, maintaining that she has done nothing
that is not wise, that therefore man must follow her, and
even if one wished to resist her it would not be possible'[7]. It is a convenient doctrine; and although it is
certainly not true that all the free-thinkers were dissolute,

it is likely that the dissolute were glad of the doctrine, in the manner of Don John and his associates in Shadwell's play *The Libertine*:—

> HERMIT. Lay by your devilish Philosophy, and change the dangerous and destructive course of your lewd lives.
>
> DON ANTONIO. Change our natures; go bid a Blackamoor be white, we follow our Constitutions, which we did not give ourselves.
>
> DON LOPEZ. What we are, we are by Nature, our reason tells us we must follow that.
>
> DON JOHN. Our Constitutions tell us one thing, and yours another; and which must we obey? If we be bad, 'tis Nature's fault, that made us so.
>
> (Act III)

That of course comes from the Restoration period (1675), though Shadwell was following traditional material. More than half a century previously Tourneur, in *The Atheist's Tragedy* (1611, or earlier), had exhibited similar muddled philosophizing in conversations between the Atheist, D'Amville, and his instrument Borachio.

> D'AMVILLE. Borachio, thou art read
> In nature and her large philosophy.
> Observ'st thou not the very self-same course
> Of revolution, both in man and beast?
> BORACHIO. The same, for birth, growth, state, decay
> and death;
> Only a man's beholding to his nature
> For the better composition of the two.
> D'AMVILLE. But where the favour of his nature is
> Not full and free, you see a man becomes
> A fool, as little-knowing as a beast.
> BORACHIO. That shows there's nothing in a man above
> His nature; if there were, considering 'tis
> His being's excellency, 'twould not yield
> To nature's weakness.

D'AMVILLE. Then, if Death cast up
  Our total sum of joy and happiness,
  Let me have all my senses feasted in
  The abundant fulness of delight at once,
  And, with a sweet insensible increase
  Of pleasing surfeit, melt into my dust.
                                              (I. i)

In the end D'Amville is caught in his own toils, and is
forced to confess,

  There was the strength of natural understanding.
  But Nature is a fool,

but his course of action throughout the play has been
rationalized in the belief

  That Nature, since herself decay doth hate,
  Should favour those that strengthen their estate.[8]

We cannot say how widespread were the sentiments
here attributed to the Atheist, but it seems likely that
Tourneur was reflecting a good deal of contemporary
discussion, some of it no doubt at a higher level of
disinterestedness than that displayed by Borachio and
pointing forward to the more painful searching of an Ivan
Karamazov ('If there is no God, everything is permitted').
To say that Shakespeare felt it as deeply significant is not
to attribute to him a greater prophetic power than
belongs to a supreme—and supremely intelligent—artist.
If the 'libertine' assumption—man is a natural force in a
world of natural forces—is incorporated in *King Lear*, that
is because it appeared to envisage nothing but the bare
facts of existence; and for Shakespeare's present purpose,
as we have seen, it was necessary to get at the bare facts.
The positives that emerge from the play are indeed
fundamentally Christian values, but they are reached by
an act of profound individual exploration: the play does
not take them for granted; it takes nothing for granted
but Nature and natural energies and passions[9].

2

The fact that *King Lear* was written so soon after
Othello (1604) is a reminder of how misleading the phrase
'Shakespearean Tragedy' can be. Each play is 'a new
beginning', a fresh 'raid on the inarticulate', for although
there is development there is no repetition. Even from
the narrowly technical point of view there are marked
differences of manner and approach between the tragedies,
corresponding to equally marked differences of intention.
Thus *Othello*, although a poetic drama, of which the
success is determined by specifically poetic effects of
language and symbolism, comes closer than any of the
other tragedies to what is commonly understood by
'revelation of character', and its focus is on individual and,
we might say, domestic qualities. *Lear*, on the other hand,
is a universal allegory (though the word 'allegory' does
justice to neither the depth nor the movement within the
experience it presents), and its dramatic technique is
determined by the need to present certain permanent
aspects of the human situation, with a maximum of
imaginative realization and a minimum regard for the
conventions of naturalism[10]. In the scenes on the
heath, for example, we do not merely listen to exchanges
between persons whom, in the course of the play, we have
got to know; we are caught up in a great and almost
impersonal poem in which we hear certain *voices* which
echo and counterpoint each other; all that they say is
part of the tormented consciousness of Lear; and the
consciousness of Lear is part of the consciousness of
human kind. There is the same density of effect throughout. One character echoes another: the blinding of
Gloucester parallels the cruelty done to Lear; Gloucester
loses his eyes, and Lear's mind is darkened; Gloucester
learns to 'see better' (as Kent had bidden Lear) in his

blindness, and Lear reaches his final insights, the recognition of his supreme need, through madness. But there is not only this mutual reinforcement *within* the play: there is constantly the felt presence of a range of experience far wider than could be attributed to any of the persons regarded simply as persons. This is achieved partly by the use of simple but effective symbols—the bare heath, the hovel, the nakedness of Poor Tom ('unaccommodated man'), the 'cliff' from which Gloucester thinks to cast himself down; partly by the use made of certain organizing ideas such as the Elizabethan conception of a necessary interrelation between man (the 'little world of man'), the social body, and the cosmos; but above all by the poetry. The poetry of *Lear* is not only vivid, close packed, and wide ranging, involving in the immediate action a world of experience, it has a peculiar resonance that should leave us in no doubt of Shakespeare's intention. It is what we hear when the blind Gloucester declares:

> I have no way, and therefore want no eyes;
> I stumbled when I saw,
>
> (IV. i. 18-19)

or when Lear, crossed by Goneril, exclaims, 'Who is it that can tell me who I am?' and the Fool replies, 'Lear's shadow' (I. iv. 238-9).

3

Lear, at the opening of the play, is the embodiment of perverse self-will. Surrounded by obsequious flattery ('They told me I was everything'), he knows neither himself nor the nature of things. It is his human self-will that is stressed, and we need not fuss very much about the apparent absurdity of his public test of his daughters' affections in the division of the kingdom. It is a dramatically heightened example of something not uncommon

—the attempt to manipulate affection which can only be freely given.

> Which of you shall we say doth love us most?
> That we our largest bounty may extend
> Where nature doth with merit challenge.*
>
> (I. i. 51-3)

To a demand of this kind the only honest reply is Cordelia's 'Nothing'. Now one result of perverse demands is a distorted view of the actual, and one way of discovering that your own lanthorn gives no light is, as Swift put it, by running your head into a post—something that is unquestionably there. Because Lear is perverse he is deceived by appearances; and because he allows himself to be deceived by appearances he sets in motion a sequence of events that finally brings him face to face with an actuality that can be neither denied nor disguised.

The subsequent action of the play is designed not only to force the hidden conflict in Lear into consciousness, and, with the fullest possible knowledge of the relevant facts, to compel a choice, but to force each one of us to confront directly the question put by Lear as Everyman, 'Who is it that can tell me who I am?' One answer to that question is embodied in the group of characters who are most directly opposed to Lear. Edmund, Goneril, and Regan take their stand on the unrestrained self-seeking of natural impulse. The two daughters, by their actions, by what they say, and by the imagery of beasts of prey so consistently associated with them[11], represent a fero-

---

* Lear's habit of arithmetical computation of degrees of affection—Coleridge's 'debtor and creditor principles of virtue'—is amusingly illustrated in Act II., scene iv., when, after he has been rebuffed by Regan, he turns to Goneril:

> I'll go with thee:
> Thy fifty yet doth double five-and-twenty,
> And thou art twice her love

94

cious animality. Their indifference to all claims but those of their own egotism is made explicit by Edmund, who brings into the play conceptions of Nature and human nature, radically opposed to the traditional conceptions, that were beginning to emerge in the consciousness of the age. For Edmund, man is merely a part of the morally indifferent world of nature, and his business is simply to assert himself with all the force and cunning at his command: 'Thou, Nature, art my goddess' (I. ii. I); 'All with me's meet that I can fashion fit' (I. ii. 191). It is into the world of indifferent natural forces, so glibly invoked by Edmund, that Lear is precipitated by a perversity of self-will that clung to the forms of human affection whilst denying the reality.

We can now see how the play at the personal or psychological level is able to bring to a focus far wider issues. Lear goes mad because he is a mind in conflict; because his conscious view of himself, to which he clings with the whole force of his personality, is irreconcilably opposed to what are in fact his basic attitudes. ' "Ay" and "no" too was no good divinity' (IV. vi. 101), and from the start there is 'division' in his 'kingdom'[12]. His talk is of love and paternal care, but both his action in casting off Cordelia and—those infallible signs of what a man truly is—his assumptions as they appear in moments of emotional stress, together with his whole tone and manner, reveal a ferocious egotism. Early in the play the contrast is more than once starkly enforced.

Here I disclaim all my paternal care,
Propinquity and property of blood,
And as a stranger to my heart and me
Hold thee from this for ever. The barbarous Scythian,
Or he that makes his generation messes
To gorge his appetite, shall to my bosom

Be as well neighbour'd, pitied, and reliev'd,
As thou my sometime daughter.

(I. i. 113-20)

Yea, is it come to this?
Let it be so: I have another daughter,
Who, I am sure, is kind and comfortable:
When she shall hear this of thee, with her nails
She'll flay thy wolvish visage.

(I. iv. 313-17)

In each of these passages the implications of the opening
lines collide sharply with what follows. Whatever Lear
thinks of himself, one side of his nature is already committed—even before he is thrust into it—to the world
that Edmund, Goneril and Regan take for granted, a
world where everything that might conceivably be
regarded as mere sentimental illusion or the product of
wishful thinking is absent, where neither 'humane
statute', custom nor religion checks the free play of brute
natural force. If Lear is ever, as Kent bids him, to 'see
better', this is the world he must see and feel in its full
impact.

The storm scenes, and the scenes immediately following, represent a two-fold process of discovery—of the
'nature' without and within. No summary can attempt
to do them justice, and perhaps the best way of indicating
what goes on in them is to revert to what has been said
of Shakespeare's superb and daring technique. The effect
is analogous to that of a symphony in which themes are
given out, developed, varied and combined. And since
one of the characters goes mad, one is an assumed madman,
and one is a Fool, there is a freedom without precedent
in the history of the drama—a freedom only limited by
the controlling purpose of the play—to press into service
all that is relevant to the full development of the main
themes.

The storm itself is vividly presented in all its power to harm[13]; but this is far from being the only way in which the action of Nature is brought home to us. Part of the dramatic function of Edgar is to reinforce the message of the storm. Disguised as one of the lowest creatures to be found in rural England in the sixteenth century (and therefore, for the purpose of the play, becoming one), a wandering madman and beggar,

> the basest and most poorest shape
> That ever penury, in contempt of man,
> Brought near to beast,

he brings with him continual reminders of rural life at its most exposed and precarious—'the winds and persecution of the sky', 'low farms, Poor pelting villages, sheep-cotes and mills' (II. iii). When Lear with Kent and the Fool surprises him in the hovel, he at once strikes the note of the familiar indifference of Nature—familiar, that is, to those who live close to nature, though not to those who, like Edmund, invoke an abstraction that suits their bent. His talk is of cold and fire, of whirlpool, whirlwind and quagmire, of natural calamity and disease. Nothing he says but has this far-reaching yet precise suggestiveness.

> Poor Tom; that eats the swimming frog, the toad, the tadpole, the wall-newt, and the water; that in the fury of his heart, when the foul fiend rages, eats cow-dung for sallets; swallows the old rat and the ditch-dog; drinks the green mantle of the standing pool . . .

> (III. iv. 132-7)

This is more than a mad fantasy of an extremity of deprivation. The effect is as though the evolutionary process had been reversed to show where man as mere earth-bred creature belongs. One recalls Timon's invocation of the earth:

G

Common mother, thou,
Whose womb unmeasurable, and infinite breast,
Teems, and feeds all; whose self-same mettle,
Whereof thy proud child, arrogant man, is puff'd,
Engenders the black toad and adder blue,
The gilded newt and eyeless venom'd worm,
With all the abhorred births below crisp heaven
Whereon Hyperion's quickening fire doth shine . . .
                    (*Timon of Athens*, IV. iii. 176-83)

Man may indeed pride himself on the achievements of civilization, riding 'proud of heart . . . on a bay trotting-horse over four-inch'd bridges' (III. iv. 56-7), but the structure is frail; it is Tom's world that endures. 'You talk of Nature', Shakespeare seems to say, 'well, take a good look at her.' 'Still through the hawthorn blows the cold wind.'

This then is the Nature 'outside'. What of human nature, the nature within? Here too the direct revelation of the action is extended and reinforced—almost overwhelmingly so—by the poetry of allusion. A long catalogue of sins—ranging from the adulteration of beer to usury, slander, perjury and murder—could be collected from the exchanges of Lear, Edgar and the Fool, and as they accumulate they give a sorry enough picture of man in his meanness. But the recurring themes are lust and cruelty. Lust and cruelty are demonstrated in the action of the play; they are harped on in Edgar's 'mad' talk; they are the horrible realities that Lear discovers beneath appearances. In the great speech beginning,

Thou rascal beadle, hold thy bloody hand!
Why dost thou lash that whore? Strip thine own
back . . .

(IV. vi. 162 ff.)

lust and sadism are—with superb insight—identified. The world of appearances is based on artificial and unreal

98

distinctions—'Robes and furr'd gowns hide all'. Strip them off and you find what Lear found in the storm.

Is man no more than this? Consider him well. Thou ow'st the worm no silk, the beast no hide, the sheep no wool, the cat no perfume. Ha! here's three on's are sophisticated; thou art the thing itself; unaccommodated man is no more but such a poor, bare, forked animal as thou art. Off, off, you lendings! Come, unbutton here. (III. iv. 105-12)

The 'thou' of that speech, the 'thing itself', is—we have just heard—'one that slept in the contriving of lust, and wak'd to do it . . . false of heart, light of ear, bloody of hand; hog in sloth, fox in stealth, wolf in greediness, dog in madness, lion in prey' (III. iv. 90-5). This, we may say, is the Edmund philosophy, though presented with a violence of realization quite foreign to the Edmund of the play. 'Lechery?' says Lear in his madness when finally broken by the storm, 'the world of nature is completely lustful. Let us admit it. Anything else is mere pretence.' 'To't, Luxury, pell-mell! For I lack soldiers' (IV. vi. 119-20)[14].

<h2 style="text-align:center">4</h2>

Lear's expression of revulsion and disgust, when, 'a ruin'd piece of nature', he confronts the blind Gloucester, is, I suppose, one of the profoundest expressions of pessimism in all literature. If it is not the final word in the play, it is certainly not because Shakespeare has shrunk from any of the issues. Pessimism is sometimes regarded as a tough and realistic attitude. Shakespeare's *total* view of human life in this play has a toughness and actuality that make most pessimism look like sentimentality. It is because the play has brought us to this vision of horror— seen without disguise or palliation—that the way is open for the final insights. In the successive stripping away of the layers of appearance, what remains to discover is the most fundamental reality of all. In the play it takes the form of the love and forgiveness of Cordelia. But that love has to be earned in the way in which all things most worth having are earned—by the full admission of a need, the achievement of honesty and humility, the painful shedding of all that is recognized as incompatible with the highest good, by, in short, making oneself able to receive whatever it may be. Now if there is one truth that the play brings home with superb force it is that neither man's reason nor his powers of perception function in isolation from the rest of his personality: *quantum sumus, scimus*[15]. *How* Lear feels, in short, is as important as *what* he feels, for the final 'seeing' is inseparable from what he has come to be. For us, as readers or spectators, Lear's vision of life can only be apprehended in close conjunction with the attitudes with which he confronts experience.

There is, of course no straight line of progress: there are developments, eddies and recessions, as the tumultuous feelings whirl into sight now one, now another aspect of what lies below the surface[16]. Although horror and rejection form the substance of Lear's last great outbursts, other feelings and other attitudes have, during the storm itself, broken through the hard crust of his will. In order to take the full force of the play's climax we must make an encircling movement, bringing into our consciousness more than can be described in objective terms of what Lear sees and suffers.

Lear's dominant attitude is obviously self-will; his sentences fall naturally into the imperative mood, his commands are threats, and his threats are curses. When crossed by Goneril he invokes Nature—Edmund's goddess —to enforce 'the untented woundings of a father's curse' (I. iv. 284 ff.); the 'Heavens' are bidden to take his part (II. iv. 163 ff., 191 ff.): and when Goneril and Regan jointly demonstrate how much power he has in fact given away his threats are vague but enormous.

> I will do such things,
> What they are, yet I know not, but they shall be
> The terrors of the earth.
>
> (II. iv. 282-4)

In all this, as Shakespeare takes care to tell us through the Fool, there is something conspicuously infantile—the craving not only for immediate gratification of his desires but for complete endorsement of the self, just as it is, the assumption of a power ludicrously beyond the possibility of performance, the resort to tantrums and tears of rage when that power proves inadequate. In these ways Lear proves his kinship with the common run of mankind long before he is prepared to admit it at a different level. Above all there is an immense capacity for self-pity. When the storm breaks self-pity joins itself incongruously to Lear's self-identification with its rage. He thinks still in terms of getting back something for what one has given: the elements are not so bad as his daughters, for they don't, like his daughters, *owe* him anything.

> I tax you not, you elements, with unkindness;
> I never gave you kingdom, call'd you children,
> You owe me no subscription: then let fall
> Your horrible pleasure; here I stand, your slave,
> A poor, infirm, weak, and despis'd old man . . .
>
> (III. ii. 16-20)

But this, like almost everything one can say about the poetry of the play, is an over-simplification. In Lear's next invocation there is very great complexity of feeling.

> Let the great gods,
> That keep this dreadful pudder o'er our heads,
> Find out their enemies now. Tremble, thou wretch,
> That hast within thee undivulged crimes,
> Unwhipp'd of Justice; hide thee, thou bloody hand,

Thou perjur'd, and thou simular of virtue
That art incestuous; caitiff, to pieces shake,
That under covert and convenient seeming
Hast practis'd on man's life; close pent-up guilts,
Rive your concealing continents, and cry
These dreadful summoners grace. I am a man
More sinn'd against than sinning.

(III. ii. 49-60)

The concern with 'undivulged crimes', with the evil that
lies below the surface, is characteristic of Lear, and is
developed later. Here it serves to distinguish between
men, who can be deceived, and 'the great Gods', who
cannot. But the implication is that the consistory of the
gods, immeasurably more powerful than its earthly counterpart (for its mere summoners are thunderbolts), is yet
like it in the exaction of merely retributive penalties.
'Unwhipp'd of justice' is indeed one of those revealing
phrases that, simply by what it takes for granted, sums
up a fundamental attitude[17]. Lear will not question the
validity of earthly justice, with its fallible ministers, nor
will he question the possibility of a more than human
justice that, though severe, has no merely punitive intention, until he has identified himself with the sinners. At
this point it is clear that he dissociates himself from those
whom the gods are required to punish, and there is even a
note of grim satisfaction as he thinks of the guilty quaking.
As the words gather momentum, culminating in the
explosive energy of

close pent-up guilts,
Rive your concealing continents. . .

it seems indeed that Lear is half-referring to himself, but
that thought is not allowed to reach full consciousness—
'I am a man More sinn'd against than sinning'. When
Kent brings him to the hovel he is still torn between the
desire for vengeance—'I will punish home'—and self-pity,

> O Regan Goneril!
> Your old kind father, whose frank heart gave all . . .

But 'that way madness lies' (III. iv. 16-21); the sore and
angry spot in his consciousness is precisely there, for
whatever his hand gave, his heart had not been as he
insists on thinking of it.

It is this warring of contradictory impulses that the
storm, a vividly evoked instance of elemental conflict,
serves to define. It is also through the storm—the storm
in the first place, and then through all the associated
images of Nature's cruelty—that reality breaks into a
mind wilfully closed against it. The question of 'true
need' has already been given some prominence (II. iv.
266-73); posed in this setting only the truth will serve.

> How dost, my boy? Art cold?
> I am cold myself. Where is this straw, my fellow?
> The art of our necessities is strange,
> And can make vile things precious. Come, your
> hovel.
>
> (III. ii. 68-71)

In a play of stark contrasts subtler shifts of tone may go
unregarded, and it is worth recalling here that earlier
question in which Lear's self-revelation came to a head—
'Which of you shall we say doth love us most?' Then the
question was asked in a tone that implied the expectation
of a gratifying answer: the leisurely and expansive rhythm
evokes the movement of settling with complacence into
prepared comfort. Now the broken rhythm marks the
confrontation of what is new and disturbing. Then the
demand was for exclusive possession, for that 'all' which
Cordelia could not pretend to give. Now what is in
question is need that must be recognized as common to
all. In the scene before the hovel, Lear's desire to share
these 'vile things' with the Fool ('In boy; go first') is,

then, shown as part of a dawning feeling for a wider human relationship. We have already heard,

> Poor Fool and knave, I have one part of my heart
> That's sorry yet for thee.

(III. ii 72-3)

Now comes the famous prayer on behalf of 'houseless poverty'.

> Poor naked wretches, whereso'er you are,
> That bide the pelting of this pitiless storm,
> How shall your houseless heads and unfed sides,
> Your loop'd and window'd raggedness, defend you
> From seasons such as these? O! I have ta'en
> Too little care of this. Take physic, Pomp;
> Expose thyself to feel what wretches feel,
> That thou mayst shake the superflux to them,
> And show the Heavens more just.

(III. iv. 28-36)

This is pity, not self-pity; and condemnation of others momentarily gives way to self-condemnation: 'O! *I* have ta'en too little care of this'. It is also, we may say, a genuine prayer, and as such it is answered: it is *after* this that Lear endures the physic of his vision of unaccommodated man.

The nature of that vision—which includes the suffering of the poor and outcast, the indifference of Nature and all the disreputable impulses that find a home in the heart of man—we have already taken some account of. From now on the question put to Lear, which is indeed the question posed by the whole play, is how to cope with the world so revealed, with the self so revealed. It can of course be said that Lear does not cope at all, since from the entrance of Poor Tom (with whom he promptly identifies himself—'Didst thou give all to thy daughters?') he is mad. What that means however is that, no longer subjected to interference from the self hitherto offered to

the world as Lear and which has proved so woefully
inadequate under stress, he is free to express attitudes
previously concealed from himself, though, as we have
seen, rather more than glimpsed by the audience. In this
region where honesty is as it were compelled—mental
and material trappings alike discarded ('Off, off, you
lendings!')—impulses issue with the uninhibited frank-
ness of the symbolic actions of dreams. At the centre of
the whirlpool lies the obsession with guilt and punishment. What constitutes the torture—Lear's 'wheel of fire'
—is that each successive attitude, bearing the stamp of its
utter inadequacy, can only breed recoil and a fresh plunge
into madness. Denial of involvement ('they cannot touch
me for coining'—IV. vi. 83) bears a confession of guilt.
Fantasies of aggression promptly transform themselves
into situations where Lear himself is the victim. Most
significant of all is the extended attempt to 'have the law
on' the offenders. But the mock trial of Goneril and
Regan (III. vi. 20-56) is not only an obliquely ironic
comment on human justice that will be made more
explicit later, it offers a direct rebuff to Lears habitual
appeal to a merely legalistic code.

> And here's another, whose warp'd looks proclaim
> What store her heart is made on. Stop her there!
> Arms, arms, sword, fire! Corruption in the place!
> False justicer, why hast thou let her 'scape?

'Corruption in the place' indeed! Lear's fantasy spins
right when, bringing the trial to an end in mad confusion,
it tells him that he cannot get at human realities in that
way.

If none of the familiar postures of the self will serve,
for the correlative of each attitude is illusion, what is
there to which Lear's mind can hold? Nothing, it seems,
except the recognition of his own share in a depravity felt
as universal. At two points indeed the recognition of his

own utter failure is not in fact accompanied by the more general reference, and these are, I think, significantly distinguished. In the first instance (IV. iii. 43 ff.) we are told about the 'shame'—the 'sovereign' and 'burning' shame—that accompanies the realization of his 'unkindness' to the daughter he had rejected. In the second, where self-accusation takes on a curiously impersonal tone, Lear himself tells how false was the flattery that he had encouraged and accepted—'They flattered me like a dog . . . When the rain came to wet me once and the wind to make me chatter, when the thunder would not peace at my bidding, there I found 'em, there I smelt 'em out' (IV. vi. 97 ff.). But although each of these passages represents a foothold in reality, although it is immediately after the first of them that Cordelia reappears, seeking her father, the nadir of Lear's vision is still to come.

5

In the two great tirades addressed to the blind Gloucester (IV. vi. 110 ff., and 151 ff.) Lear brings to a head all he has discovered concerning Appetite and Authority. The discovery is that appetite is well nigh universal and that authority is a sham. For the man who knows this, who knows too how little he can dissociate himself from what he denounces, aggression and self-assertion are alike irrelevant: all that is left is a 'patience' hardly distinguishable from despair.

> Thou must be patient; we came crying hither:
> Thou know'st the first time that we smell the air
> We wawl and cry. I will preach to thee: mark . . .
> When we are born, we cry that we are come
> To this great stage of fools.

> (IV. vi. 180-5)

There is no immediate way of deciding how we should take these lines. It is important that we should know since it is virtually on this note (after a momentary return to a futile fantasy of revenge) that Lear gives way completely, sleeps, and is carried to Cordelia. The question is whether what we have here is a weary subsidence into the only wisdom that is ultimately possible, or whether, although representing an extreme point of weariness and denial, it masks the possibility of some genuine resilience of the spirit. In order to determine this we must recall the familiar truth that dramatic statements exist in a context, and that their meaning is in relation to—often in tension with—that context. Lear is indeed the central consciousness of the play, but nothing, so far, has put us under any compulsion to accept him as solely qualified as an interpreter of the action. At this point then we must briefly recall the part played by Gloucester, the Fool, Kent, and some others.

Both Gloucester and the Fool powerfully affect our sense of the central experience embodied in Lear, but they belong to two quite different aspects of Shakespeare's wide-embracing dramatic technique. The Gloucester sub-plot is plainly 'a device of intensification'[18], and the progress of Gloucester himself is something like a simplified projection of the Lear experience on to a 'morality' plane: in the bewildering world of the play it helps to give us our bearings. It is commonly recognized that just as Lear finds 'reason in madness' (IV. vi. 177) so Gloucester learns to 'see' in his blindness, and there is no need to rehearse the many parallels of situation, the verbal echoes and cross-references. All that concerns us here can be plainly stated. Gloucester, at the beginning of the play, is sufficiently characterized by his coarse man-of-the-world conversation; he is as blind as Lear to the truth of things, credulous and, one would have said, ineffective. Caught up in the struggle of good and evil his decision to help Lear is deliberate and heroic—'If I die for it, as no less is threat-

ened me, the King, my old master, must be reliev'd'
(III. iii. 18-20)—and his blinding is a kind of martyrdom.
It is a martyrdom, however, from which any consolatory
vision is completely absent, and his subsequent progress,
always so close to despair, is deliberately deprived of
any obvious 'nobility' matching his conduct—as in the
grotesque comedy of his attempted suicide[19]. But it is
Shakespeare's refusal to romanticize Gloucester that so
guarantees the validity of the qualities with which he is
endowed. Gloucester learns to suffer, to feel, and in feeling
to see; and under Edgar's guidance he comes as near as he
may to thoughts that are not only 'patient' but 'free'[20].
At that point in the play which, it may be recalled, this
consideration of Gloucester is intended to bear on, he has
yet to undergo further vicissitudes of feeling—the 'ill
thoughts' with which Edgar taxes him (v. ii. 9)—before,
reconciled to the son who has saved him from 'despair',
his heart bursts 'smilingly', "twixt . . . joy and grief'
(v. iii. 188-99). But we have been left in no doubt of what
he contributes to the play. The Gloucester who listens to
Lear's tirades is someone quite other than his earlier self,
someone incredibly—miraculously, the play suggests*—
better. And the change in him, defined and emphasized
by the touching simplicity of the verse he speaks, is
something that our imagination completely endorses[21].

The nature of Gloucester's experience is clearly presented, without ambiguity. The Fool, on the other hand,
speaks to (and out of) a quite different order of apprehension: his function is to disturb with glimpses of confound-
ing truths that elude rational formulation. At times he
seems like something only partly recognized in the depths
of Lear's own personality that will not be kept down

* Thy life's a miracle (iv. vi. 55)
Think that the clearest Gods, who make them honours
Of men's impossibilities, have preserved thee.   (iv. vi. 73-4)

('Take heed, sirrah; the whip'), but because he is only licensed, not enfranchised—not, we may say, integrated with the conscious self, which yet has a vein of tenderness towards him—the truth he tells is disguised, paradoxical, sometimes grotesque. He *looks towards* Cordelia, pining when she is banished and slipping out of the play before her reappearance; at the end there is some confusion in Lear's mind between the two (v. iii. 305)[22]. Miss Welsford, in the penetrating account she gives of him in her book, *The Fool*, places him firmly in the tradition of 'the sage-fool who sees the truth' ('his rôle', she adds, 'has even more *intellectual* than emotional significance')[23]. The truths he tells are of various kinds. He can formulate the tenets of worldly wisdom with a clarity that worldly wisdom often prefers to blur. He defines the predatory self-seeking of Goneril and Regan, and has a variety of pithy phrases both for the outward form of Lear's mistaken choice and its hidden causes and results. In relation to these last indeed he shows an uncanny insight, pointing directly to Lear's infantile craving 'to make his daughters his mothers' (i. iv. 179-81), and hinting at that element of dissociated sexuality that plays into so many human disorders—something that will later rise to the surface of Lear's mind with obsessive force. The world picture he creates is of small creatures in a world too big—and, in its human aspects, too bad— to be anything but bewildering. His sharply realistic, commonplace instances—like Tom's mad talk, though with a different tone—insist on the alien aspect of Nature and on all that detracts from man's sense of his own dignity—corns, chilblains, lice, and the mere pricking of sexual desire. The Fool's meaning, however, lies not merely in what he says but in the way he says it—those riddling snatches which partly reflect the moral confusion of the world, but whose main function is to cast doubt on such certainties as the world (including the audience) thinks it possesses. Not only therefore is he an agent of clarification, prompting Lear towards the recognition of bitter truths: it is he, as Miss Welsford insists, who forces the question, What is wisdom? and what is folly? It is through him, therefore, that we come to see more clearly the sharp distinction between those whose wisdom is purely for themselves and those foolish ones—Kent, Gloucester, Cordelia, and the Fool himself—who recklessly take their stand on loyalties and sympathies that are quite outside the scope of any prudential calculus. Like Gloucester, though in a very different way, the Fool is directed towards an affirmation.

Both the Fool and Gloucester stand in a peculiarly close relation to Lear, but whereas the Fool is inseparable from him, Gloucester also connects with a wider world—a world existing independently of Lear's own consciousness (the alternation of scenes throughout Act III has great dramatic force and significance). Now that world has so far been dominated by those active promoters of their own fortunes, Goneril, Regan, Edmund and Cornwall, but Shakespeare has also included in it quite other types of representative humanity. Kent, who follows Lear without coming close to him like the Fool or sharing something of the inner nature of his experience like Gloucester, has an especially significant rôle. Even in a play that is far from naturalistic we are bound to reflect that a king who could inspire the dogged devotion of such a man must be remarkable for something else besides perversity: his mere presence helps to check such inclination as we might harbour to regard Lear as foolish and wilful in such wildly improbable ways that we can safely dissociate ourselves[24]. And his headstrong loyalty is a reminder of certain permanent possibilities of human nature. Moreover fellow-feeling, loyalty, even sacrifice are not confined to the more conspicuous figures. It is a mere serving-man who gives his life in a vain attempt to save Gloucester; another fetches 'flax and whites of eggs To apply to his bleeding face', and, with a fellow, is allowed to act as final chorus to that monstrous scene (III. vii. 71-106); and there is the Old Man, tenant of the Gloucesters 'these fourscore years', who leads Gloucester to Poor Tom, then goes to fetch for 'the naked fellow' 'the best 'parel' that he has—'Come on't what will' (IV. i. 10-50). These also play their part on Lear's 'great stage'.

Even apart from the central movement of Lear's own consciousness, therefore, the development of the play as a whole towards the last great outburst of his pessimism is very far indeed from a simple descent through deepening horrors that would justify an unqualified endorsement of his rejection of the world. There is indeed a full and passionate confrontation of 'the worst', including Edgar's recognition that there is no term that can be set to suffering (IV. i. 24). But not only does the play compel our recognition of positive values and emerging insights, the same ruthless honesty that has stripped Lear of every rag of illusion is directed also to the brutal 'realism' of his opponents. It is indeed in the fourth act that the mutual treachery of competing egotisms begins to reveal itself (IV. ii., IV. v., IV. vi. 258 ff.), and the logic of events underlines the penetrating explicitness of Albany's judgment of Goneril:

> O Goneril!
> You are not worth the dust which the rude wind
> Blows in your face . . .
> That nature, which contemns its origin,
> Cannot be border'd certain in itself;
> She that herself will sliver and disbranch
> From her material sap, perforce must wither

And come to deadly use . . .
If that the heavens do not their visible spirits
Send quickly down to tame these vilde offences,
It will come,
Humanity must perforce prey on itself,
Like monsters of the deep.

(IV. ii. 30 ff.)

When, therefore, Lear 'preaches' to Gloucester on the vanity of human life, there is, as so often in Shakespeare, a clash between the personal or immediate meaning of the words and their full dramatic meaning.

. . . we came crying hither:
Thou know'st the first time that we smell the air
We wawl and cry . . .
When we are born, we cry that we are come
To this great stage of fools.

The force and bitterness of 'this great stage of fools' takes this far beyond the accepted commonplaces on the new born infant's tears[25]: for Lear, at this point, life is a meaningless comedy of pain. But no more than Macbeth's 'Life is a tale told by an idiot' can this be regarded simply as a summarizing comment emerging from the play as a whole. To be sure the accumulated meaning of the play puts sufficient weight behind the bitterness, but the whole relevant context forbids a simple response. The context of course is not something 'out there' that can be demonstrated in terms of the understanding, it is all that our minds and imaginations, awakened and directed by Shakespeare's art, hold ready to receive and interpret the immediate situation. And what our imaginations now hold is not only a sense of Lear's folly and suffering, of the folly, suffering, cruelty and injustice to be found in the world at large, but a heightened recognition of all that, even in the face of these, the whole personality endorses as clear insight and genuinely human feeling. And behind the widening circle of reference within the play itself there is a context even more extensive. This indeed is slippery ground for interpretation, but it is at least relevant to recall that in other plays of roughly the same period—notably perhaps in *Timon of Athens*, so close to *Lear* in its probing of certain moods of revulsion—Shakespeare was concerned with the way in which the world of the individual is in part created by the non-rational structure of attitudes and feelings that are inseparable from perception. Only an inhibiting fear of life could prevent us from taking the full force of Lear's great indictment: only a refusal to meet honestly—so far as we may—*all* that Shakespeare sets in relation to it could make us blind to the irony—yes, even in this moment of keenest suffering—that plays about it.

What then are the reflections that, with a reversal of the usual effect of dramatic irony, qualify our recognition of all that is valid in Lear's bitterness? Surely they include such thoughts as that the image Lear finds for the world is partly at least a projection of his own folly; that not all the inhabitants of Lear's world are fools in the sense immediately intended here; that folly is a word whose meaning changes according to the standpoint of the speaker, and that in the pain of madness Lear had at least learnt more about human nature than he knew before. With this we bring into focus the three times repeated reference to the birth-cry. Whatever the physiological reasons, the baby's cry at smelling the air (and nothing can deprive that phrase of its disturbing wholesomeness) is commonly taken as a cry of fright and protest—'Helpless, naked, piping loud'. As such it is analogous to the protest, the frightened movement towards headlong regression, of the adult who is called upon to undergo a radical transformation of consciousness. In the subtle and complex interplay of recognitions that surrounds our sympathy with Lear's agony this thought also has its place.

6

It is through such varied probings, questionings, rejections, recognitions, that a direction is established and a way prepared. Cordelia, though rarely appearing in the play, is very much a positive presence. Her tenderness is rooted in the same strength that enabled her to reject Lear's misconceived demands. Her love is of a kind that, confronted with a real demand, does not bargain or make conditions; it is freely given, and it represents an absolute of human experience that can stand against the full shock of disillusion. When Lear, dressed in 'fresh garments' and to the accompaniment of music (the symbolism is important) is brought into her presence, there follows one of the most tender and moving scenes in the whole of Shakespeare. But it is much more than moving. Since each line engages us to the whole extent of our powers the briefest reminders set vibrating all the chords of the past experience. It is even whilst we respond to the swift sure play of feeling—with a sense as of the actual bodily presence of the protagonists[26]—that we are made to live again the central scenes.

> CORDELIA. O my dear father! Restoration hang
>   Thy medicine on my lips, and let this kiss
>   Repair those violent harms that my two sisters
>   Have in thy reverence made
> KENT.   Kind and dear Princess!
> CORDELIA. Had you not been their father, these white
>   flakes
>   Did challenge pity of them. Was this a face
>   To be oppos'd against the warring winds?
>   To stand against the deep dread-bolted thunder?
>   In the most terrible and nimble stroke

Of quick, cross lightning? to watch—poor *perdu*!—
With this thin helm? Mine enemy's dog,
Though he had bit me, should have stood that night
Against my fire. And wast thou fain, poor father,
To hovel thee with swine and rogues forlorn,
In short and musty straw? Alack, alack!
'Tis wonder that thy life and wits at once
Had not concluded all . . .

                                        (IV. vii. 26-42)

Hence as recognition dawns in Lear, as consciousness first renews his suffering, then admits it has no terms for a world not known before, we are aware that this still moment is surrounded by nothing less than the whole action of the play; and if questions that have been asked now await their answer, the painful knowledge that has been won will reject anything that swerves a hair's breadth from absolute integrity.

CORDELIA.   He wakes; speak to him.
DOCTOR. Madam, do you; 'tis fittest.
CORDELIA. How does my royal Lord? How fares your
    Majesty?
LEAR. You do me wrong to take me out o' th' grave;
    Thou art a soul in bliss; but I am bound
    Upon a wheel of fire, that mine own tears
    Do scald like molten lead.
CORDELIA.   Sir, do you know me?
LEAR. You are a spirit, I know; where did you die?
CORDELIA. Still, still, far wide.
DOCTOR. He's scarce awake; let him alone awhile.
LEAR. Where have I been? Where am I? Fair daylight?
    I am mightily abus'd. I should e'en die with pity
    To see another thus. I know not what to say.
    I will not swear these are my hands: let's see;
    I feel this pin prick. Would I were assur'd
    Of my condition!

115

CORDELIA. O! look upon me, Sir,
And hold your hand in benediction o'er me.
No, Sir, you must not kneel.

LEAR. Pray, do not mock me:
I am a very foolish fond old man,
Fourscore and upward, not an hour more or less;
And, to deal plainly,
I fear I am not in my perfect mind.
Methinks I should know you and know this man;
Yet I am doubtful: for I am mainly ignorant
What place this is, and all the skill I have
Remembers not these garments; nor I know not
Where I did lodge last night. Do not laugh at me;
For, as I am a man, I think this lady
To be my child Cordelia.

CORDELIA. And so I am, I am.

LEAR. Be your tears wet? Yes, faith. I pray, weep not;
If you have poison for me, I will drink it.
I know you do not love me; for your sisters
Have, as I do remember, done me wrong:
You have some cause, they have not.

CORDELIA. No cause, no cause.

LEAR. Am I in France?

KENT. In your own kindgom, Sir.

(IV. vii. 42-76)

It is in the light of everything that has gone before that
we recognize this as a moment of truth.

King Lear, however, is more than a purgatorial experience culminating in reconciliation: what it does in fact
culminate in we know, and the play's irony, its power to
disturb, is sustained. Does this mean, then, that *King Lear*
is 'a sublime question, to which no answer is supplied by
the play'?[27] I do not think so. What it does mean is that
questioning, disturbance, the absence of demonstrable
answers, form an essential part of a meaning that lies not
in a detachable moral but in the activity and wholeness of

116

the imagination. To the extent therefore that *King Lear* does make a positive affirmation (and I think it does) it is one which takes up into itself the questioning: it is an affirmation 'in spite of' [28].

In the last act, by the definite withdrawal of Albany from the forces opposed to Lear, the killing of Edmund by Edgar in single combat, and the mutual treachery of Goneril and Regan, the way is apparently cleared for an ending far different from that represented by the stark stage-direction: 'Enter Lear, with Cordelia dead in his arms'. The scene of Lear's final anguish is so painful that criticism hesitates to fumble with it: where no one can remain unaffected the critic's business is to supply something other than his own emotions. What may be said, however, is that there are at least two reasons why no other ending would have been imaginatively right, and for a proper understanding they are of the greatest importance. We do not only look at a masterpiece, we enter into it and live with it. Our suffering, then, and our acceptance of suffering, not simply our sympathy with what we see on the stage, form an intrinsic part of what the play is; for as with Lear and Gloucester our capacity to see is dependent upon our capacity to feel. Now what our seeing has been directed towards is nothing less than *what man is*. The imaginative discovery that is the play's essence has thus involved the sharpest possible juxtaposition of rival conceptions of 'Nature'. In the Edmund-Goneril-Regan group the philosophy of natural impulse and egotism has been revealed as self-consuming, its claim to represent strength as a self-bred delusion. What Lear touches in Cordelia, on the other hand, is, we are made to feel, the reality, and the values revealed so surely there are established in the face of the worst that can be known of man or Nature. To keep nothing in reserve, to slur over no possible cruelty or misfortune, was the only way

of ensuring that the positive values discovered and established in the play should keep their triumphant hold on
our imagination, should assert that unconditional rightness which, in any full and responsive reading of *King
Lear*, we are bound to attribute to them.

★   ★   ★

Perhaps a final question remains. It has been argued here
that at the centre of the action is the complete endorsement of a particular quality of being. We may call it love
so long as we remember that it is not simply an emotion,
and that, although deeply personal, it has also the impersonality that comes from a self-forgetful concentration—
momentary or enduring—upon the true being of 'the
other': it is perhaps this kind of impersonality—not a
negation of personal consciousness but its heightening and
fulfilment—that is most insisted on in Edgar's strange
phrase, 'Ripeness is all' (v. ii. 11). In this sense—so the
play reveals—love is that without which life is a meaningless chaos of competing egotisms; it is the condition of
intellectual clarity, the energizing centre from which
personality may grow unhampered by the need for self-
assertion or evasive subterfuge; it is the sole ground of a
genuinely self-affirming life and energy. But—it may still
be asked—how does this apply to Lear when he prattles
to Cordelia about gilded butterflies, or when, thinking
his dead daughter is alive, his heart breaks at last? For
answer, we must consider once more the play's marvellous technique, the particular way in which it enlivens
and controls our sympathies and perceptions. King Lear
is indeed, for most of the play, 'the centre of consciousness': what he sees we are forced to see. But the question,
ultimately, is not what Lear sees but what Shakespeare
sees, and what we, as audience, are prompted to see with
him. At the end, however poignantly we may feel—Lear's

118

suffering is one of the permanent possibilities, and we know it—we are still concerned with nothing less than the inclusive vision of the whole; and it is that which justifies us in asserting that the mind, the imagination, so revealed is directed towards affirmation *in spite of everything*. Other readings of the play are possible, and have been made. But those who think that it is 'pessimistic', that it is no more than a deeply moving contemplation of man's helplessness, should consider a remarkable and obvious fact: that the tragedies written after *King Lear* everywhere proclaim an intellectual and imaginative energy that, in the firmness of its grasp, the assurance of its sense of life, shows no sign of perplexity, fear, or strain. For what takes place in *King Lear* we can find no other word than renewal.

CHAPTER VI

Macbeth

I

MACBETH defines a particular kind of evil—the evil that results from a lust for power. The defining, as in all the tragedies, is in strictly poetic and dramatic terms. It is certainly not an abstract formulation, but lies rather in the drawing out of necessary consequences and implications of that lust both in the external and the spiritual worlds. Its meaning, therefore, is revealed in the expansion and unfolding of what lies within the initial evil, in terms of direct human experience. The logic is not formal but experiential, and demands from us, if we are to test its validity and feel its force, a fulness of imaginative response and a closeness of realization, in which both sensation and feeling become modes of understanding. Only when intellect, emotion, and a kind of direct sensory awareness work together can we enter fully into that exploratory and defining process.

In other words, the essential structure of *Macbeth*, as of the other tragedies, is to be sought in the poetry. That of course is easily said; what it means is something that can only be grasped in relation to specific instances or not grasped at all. We may take as an example Macbeth's 'aside' when he has been greeted as Thane of Cawdor.

> This supernatural soliciting
> Cannot be ill; cannot be good:—
> If ill, why hath it given me earnest of success,
> Commencing in a truth? I am thane of Cawdor:
> If good, why do I yield to that suggestion

Whose horrid image doth unfix my hair,
And make my seated heart knock at my ribs,
Against the use of nature? Present fears
Are less than horrible imaginings.
My thought, whose murder yet is but fantastical,
Shakes so my single state of man,
That function is smother'd in surmise,
And nothing is, but what is not.

(I. iii. 130-42)

This is temptation, presented with concrete force. Even if we attend only to the revelation of Macbeth's spiritual state, our recognition of the body—the very feel—of the experience, is a response to the poetry, to such things as the sickening see-saw rhythm ('Cannot be ill; cannot be good . . .') changing to the rhythm of the pounding heart, the over-riding of grammar ('My thought, whose murder yet is but fantastical') as thought is revealed in the very process of formation, and so on. But the poetry makes further claims, and if we attend to them we find that the words do not only point inward to the presumed state of Macbeth's mind but, as it were, outward to the play as a whole. The equivocal nature of temptation, the commerce with phantoms consequent upon false choice, the resulting sense of unreality ('nothing is, but what is not'), which has yet such power to 'smother' vital function, the unnaturalness of evil ('against the use of nature'), and the relation between disintegration in the individual ('my single state of man') and disorder in the larger social organism—all these are major themes of the play which are mirrored in the speech under consideration. They emerge as themes because they are what the poetry— reinforced by action and symbolism—again and again insists on. And the interrelations we are forced to make take us outside the speeches of the protagonist to the poetry of the play as a whole. That 'smother'd', for example, takes us forward not only to Lady Macbeth's 'blanket of the dark' but to such things as Rosse's choric comment after the murder of Duncan:—

by th' clock 'tis day,
And yet dark night strangles the travelling lamp.
Is't night's predominance, or the day's shame,
That darkness does the face of earth entomb,
When living light should kiss it?

(ii. iv. 6-10)

In none of the tragedies is there anything superfluous, but it is perhaps *Macbeth* that gives the keenest impression of economy. The action moves directly and quickly to the crisis, and from the crisis to the full working out of plot and theme. The pattern is far easier to grasp than that of *Lear*. The main theme of the reversal of values is given out simply and clearly in the first scene—'Fair is foul, and foul is fair'; and with it are associated premonitions of the conflict, disorder and moral darkness into which Macbeth will plunge himself. Well before the end of the first act we are in possession not only of the positive values against which the Macbeth evil will be defined but of the related aspects of that evil, which is simultaneously felt as a strained and unnatural perversion of the will, an obfuscation of the clear light of reason, a principle of disorder (both in the 'single state of man' and in his wider social relations), and a pursuit of illusions. All these impressions, which as the play proceeds assume the status of organizing ideas, are produced by the inter-action of all the resources of poetic drama—action, contrast, statement, implication, imagery and allusion. Thus the sense of the unnaturalness of evil is evoked not only by repeated explicit references ('nature's mischief', 'nature seems dead', ''Tis unnatural, even like the deed that's done', and so on) but by the expression of unnatural sentiments and an unnatural violence of tone in such things as Lady Macbeth's invocation of the 'spirits' who will 'unsex' her, and her affirmation that she would murder the babe at her breast if she had sworn to do it. So too the theme of the false appearances inseparable from evil, of deceit recoiling on the deceiver, is not only the subject of explicit comment

—And be these juggling fiends no more believ'd,
That palter with us in a double sense—

(v. viii. 19-20)

it is embodied in the action, so that Macbeth's despairing recognition of mere 'mouth-honour' among his remaining followers (v. iii. 27) echoes ironically his wife's advice to 'look like th' innocent flower, But be the serpent under't' (I. v. 64-5) and the hypocritical play of the welcoming of Duncan; and it is reinforced by—or indeed one with—the evoked sense of equivocation and evasiveness associated with the witches, and the cloud of uncertainty that settles on Scotland during Macbeth's despotism. It is fitting that the final movement of the reversal that takes place in the last act should open with the command of Malcolm to the camouflaged soldiers, 'Your leavy screens throw down, And show like those you are' (v. vi. 1-2).

2

The assurance of *Macbeth* has behind it, is indeed based on, a deeply imagined resolution of perplexities inherent in any full exposure to life. Freedom from the tyranny of time and illusion is finally related, at the deepest levels of consciousness, to the central affirmations of the spirit; and conversely, the obsessed awareness of time without meaning, like the subjection of mind to appearance, is revealed not simply as consequential on false choice but as intrinsic to it: for 'the eye altering alters all'. There is a similar assurance in the use of 'nature', in that aspect of the play's imaginative structure that impels us to say not merely that Macbeth's crime is unnatural (*i.e.* inhuman) but that the values against which evil is defined are in some sense grounded in nature. To suggest how this is so, to relate the insights operative here to those already touched on, it is necessary to step back from the play and to see it in the wider context of Shakespeare's development as a whole. Although in recent years much has been written about the meanings of nature in Shakespeare and his contemporaries[1], there is still need for further clarification of the perceptions controlling the use of this elusive, indispensable and pregnant word.

In Shakespeare's poetic thought we find two apparently contradictory intuitions regarding man's relation to the created world existing independently of human choice and will. Nature and human values are felt as intimately related, and at the same time as antagonistic.

They are related in two ways. Shakespeare, like almost all poets, uses natural imagery to evoke and define qualities that are humanly valuable, indeed indispensable to any full humanity:

> She that herself will sliver and disbranch
> From her material sap, perforce must wither
> And come to deadly use.

> For his bounty,
> There was no winter in't; an autumn 'twas
> That grew the more by reaping.

These are striking instances, but in even apparently casual metaphors and similes—'my love is all as boundless as the sea', 'and she in thee Calls back the lovely April of her prime', 'as dear to me as are the ruddy drops That visit my sad heart'—it seems that we have to do with a relationship more intimate than that of mere resemblance: the mind has in some sense *found itself* in nature; for, as Leone Vivante says of Shakespeare's images of budding and of morning, 'the grace of things in their birth and their first purity would not be perceived, if it were not *first* a quality of our mental synthesis which is revealed in and through them'[2]. This is indeed a truth of general application; Blake's Tiger, Herbert's Flower, Marvell's Garden (in the poems of those names), and Wordsworth's

> uncertain heaven, received
> Into the bosom of the steady lake,
> *(The Prelude*, v. 387-8)

all imply a basic kinship of human and non-human life: mind would be less truly itself if it were not deeply responsive to images such as these. The correspondences between mind and natural forms and natural processes is attested by common speech as well as by the poets. Just as it is with peculiar rightness that George Herbert can say, 'And now in age I bud again', or that Marvell can speak of 'a green thought in a green shade', so images of budding, growing, harvesting, of night, dawn and day, of seasons and weathers, of climates and landscapes, are integral to the speech in which we ourselves feel after inner experience.

> *La Nature est un temple où de vivants piliers*
> *Laissent parfois sortir de confuses paroles;*
> *L'homme y passe à travers des forêts de symboles*
> *Qui l'observent avec des regards familiers.*[3]

In Shakespeare there is no attempt to explain the working of these *regards familiers*; but the mere fact that his plays and poems are full of these more-than-analogies implies that psychic life is at home in nature.

But even if we leave aside the difficult question of natural symbolism, there is no doubt that wherever Shakespeare envisages a fully human way of life he thinks of it as closely related to the wider setting of organic growth, as indeed, in a quite concrete and practical way,

directly based on man's dealings with the earth that
nourishes him. It is of course in *The Winter's Tale* that we
are most explicitly aware of nature as a powerful controlling presence[4]—a presence moreover not vaguely felt
but specifically rendered in the great pastoral scene with
its many reminders of seasonal activities, humble in themselves but translucent to the great myths. But Shakespeare's
vision of the intimate relationship between man and
nature, of nature as the necessary basis and, under certain
conditions, the pattern for civilization, goes back to the
period before the final plays and before the tragedies. It is
expressed in the beautiful but strangely neglected speech
of Burgundy, in *King Henry V*, when he urges peace.

> . . . let it not disgrace me
> If I demand before this royal view,
> Why that the naked, poor, and mangled Peace,
> Dear nurse of arts, plenties, and joyful births,
> Should not in this best garden of the world,
> Our fertile France, put up her lovely visage?
> Alas! she hath from France too long been chas'd,
> And all her husbandry doth lie on heaps,
> Corrupting in its own fertility.
> Her vine, the merry cheerer of the heart,
> Unpruned dies; her hedges even-pleach'd
> Like prisoners wildly overgrown with hair,
> Put forth disorder'd twigs; her fallow leas
> The darnel, hemlock and rank fumitory
> Doth root upon, while that the coulter rusts
> That should deracinate such savagery;
> The even mead, that erst brought sweetly forth
> The freckled cowslip, burnet, and green clover,
> Wanting the scythe, all uncorrected, rank,
> Conceives by idleness, and nothing teems
> But hateful docks, rough thistles, kecksies, burrs,
> Losing both beauty and utility.
> And as our vineyards, fallows, meads, and hedges,

Defective in their natures, grow to wildness,
Even so our houses and ourselves and children
Have lost, or do not learn for want of time,
The sciences that should become our country,
But grow like savages, as soldiers will
That nothing do but meditate on blood,
To swearing and stern looks, defus'd attire,
And every thing that seems unnatural.

(v. ii. 31-62)

There is here an imaginative vision that transcends the simple sequence of the argument. After the preliminary invocation of peace the passage is built on a simple inversion: uncultivated nature ('corrupting in its own fertility' —a phrase that Milton must have remembered) is compared to disorderly or uncultivated human life, which in turn is compared to 'wild' or 'savage' nature. But what we have to deal with is something more complex than a simple comparison which is then given again with the terms reversed; Burgundy is throughout expressing a sense of the interrelationship—a two-way traffic— between man and nature. Natural fertility ('our fertile France') is the necessary precondition not only of life at the biological level but of the highest reaches of man-made civilization—the 'arts' and 'sciences' (both of which can be interpreted in the widest sense); whilst at the same time, since peace is the nurse not only of these but of all that comes to birth, of the very fertility on which the whole range of human activity depends, and since it is man who *makes* peace, man is responsible for nature. The alternative to peace is 'wildness' in both man and nature, and for man to tame that wildness in himself is a process analogous to taming what is given in external nature. So much is stated or directly suggested: what is not quite explicit but imaginatively present, adding life and vibrancy to the flat prose-meaning to which I have reduced the poetry, is the vision of peace. Conceived throughout as a wholesome *activity*—'laying' hedges, ploughing, and so on are taken as representative examples —it is a state in which arts and sciences and daily beauty and utility are conceived both as end and as condition of the fertility on which all alike depend. Behind the image of life and nature run wild for lack of human care is the implied ideal of natural force tended and integrated into a truly human civilization. And the inclusive 'Peace', teeming with human activity, is the 'natural' end of the 'joyful births': it is the alternative 'wildness' that is 'unnatural'.

But if Burgundy's speech, looking forward as it does to *The Winter's Tale*, represents an important element in Shakespeare's imaginative vision of man and nature, there is also another, its polar opposite, of which a brief reminder will serve. If nature is bounty she is also decay; she is the ally of chance in 'untrimming' 'every fair' (Sonnet XVIII); it is the same sky that indifferently 'cheers' and 'checks' both men and flowers (Sonnet XV). Worse still, if nature as the world of organic growth and decay is indifferent to human needs, as instinct and appetite ('blood') she can be positively hostile to the life of the spirit. And between 'natural law' as traditionally understood (*i.e.*, reason) and the law of nature by which, as Falstaff lightly remarked, the young dace is a bait for the old pike, there is an absolute distinction.

All this Shakespeare knew well enough, and in *King Lear*, addressing himself to the question of man's place in nature, and with a full view of all the potential evil in man as part of nature, he magnificently re-affirmed the autonomy of the spirit. Yet in Shakespeare's poetic thought the idea of relationship to nature seems as integral as the idea of the fundamental difference between the two realms. The question we are forced to ask, therefore, is, If human nature is not entirely at home in the world of

nature, if in some essential ways it is set over against
nature, how can mind find itself in nature, as there is such
abundant testimony that it does? How is it that in
Macbeth (to be specific) essential distinctions of good and
evil, belonging to the inner world, can be defined in
imagery of the outer world of nature, defined moreover
in such a way that the imaginative correspondence goes
far beyond the use of selected analogies and implies a
symbolic equivalence—indeed a relationship—between
what is 'natural' for man and what is 'natural' in the
simplest and widest sense of the word?[5]

We are led back once more to *King Lear*, to one scene
in particular where we first become conscious of a change
in direction of the imaginative current of the play, as
though a slight but unmistakable breeze were announcing
that a tide, still at the ebb, is about to turn. In the
opening scenes of Act IV the worst is still to come; both
Gloucester and Lear have still to reach the lowest point of
their despair. But Gloucester, we know, is in the care of
Edgar, and in the fourth scene, immediately after we have
been told of Lear's purgatorial shame, Cordelia enters,
'with drum and colours', seeking her father.

> CORDELIA. Alack! 'tis he: why, he was met even now
> As mad as the vex'd sea; singing aloud;
> Crown'd with rank fumiter and furrow-weeds,
> With hardocks, hemlock, nettles, cuckoo-flowers,
> Darnel, and all the idle weeds that grow
> In our sustaining corn. A century send forth;
> Search every acre in the high-grown field,
> And bring him to our eye. [*Exit* AN OFFICER.]
>   What can man's wisdom
> In the restoring his bereaved sense?
> He that helps him take all my outward worth.
> DOCTOR. There is means, madam;
> Our foster-nurse of nature is repose,

The which he lacks; that to provoke in him,
Are many simples operative, whose power
Will close the eye of anguish.

CORDELIA.   All bless'd secrets,
All you unpublish'd virtues of the earth,
Spring with my tears! be aidant and remediate
In the good man's distress! Seek, seek for him,
Lest his ungovern'd rage dissolve the life
That wants the means to lead it.

(IV. iv. 1-20)

What is remarkable here is the particular quality of the awareness of nature that lies behind and informs the poetry. Lear's 'ungovern'd rage' is compared, as before, to elemental fury ('as mad as the vex'd sea'), and his mock crown is fittingly made up of 'idle weeds', astonishingly present in the clogged movement of the lines that list them. Yet co-present with these—and given emphasis by the lift and smooth sweep of the verse—is 'our sustaining corn'; and the same earth bears the medicinal plants that foster restoring sleep ('balm of hurt minds, great nature's second course')[6]. Nature, then, is contemplated in both its aspects, as that which preserves and as that which impedes, encroaches on or rises in turmoil against man's specifically human activities; and it is contemplated with a peculiar serenity. It is of course contemplated from the standpoint of Cordelia; and her qualities—those particularly that lie behind this serenity —have been explicitly and beautifully evoked in the immediately preceding scene. The law of her nature, it is clear, is quite other than the law of nature to which Goneril and Regan abandon themselves:—

it seem'd she was a queen
Over her passion; who, most rebel-like,
Sought to be king o'er her.

(IV. iii. 14-16)

Yet there is nothing rigid in this self-control. She is mov'd, though 'not to a rage'; and we feel it fitting that one so far removed from all that is merely natural should yet attract to herself images and associations from the world of nature,

> . . . patience and sorrow strove
> Who should express her goodliest. You have seen
> Sunshine and rain at once; her smiles and tears
> Were like, a better way,
>
> (IV. iii. 18-20)

just as it is perfectly in keeping that religious associations —'There she shook The holy water from her heavenly eyes' (IV. iii. 30-1)—should almost immediately blend with those of 'sunshine and rain at once'[7]. What we are given in the poetry is a sure and sensitive poise, and it is Cordelia's integrity—her tenderness, as we have seen, at one with her strength—that explains her full and ready responsiveness. It is because she is fully human—though there are also potent suggestions of divine grace—that she is 'natural' in a different sense from that intended in Edmund's philosophy. Her sense of the bounty of nature ('of our sustaining corn' as well as of the 'rank fumiter and furrow-weeds') lies behind her invocation,—

> All bless'd secrets,
> All you unpublish'd virtues of the earth,
> Spring with my tears! be aidant and remediate
> In the good man's distress!

But it is because of her love and pity ('the good man' is the erring Lear) that she can invoke so whole-heartedly the 'unpublish'd virtues of the earth'—can invoke them moreover not simply as allies from a different realm, but with a suggestion of kinship and intimacy that almost equates their working with the power of out-going and healing life that lies deep in the soul[8]. It is in this sense that Cordelia 'redeems nature from the general curse Which twain have brought her to' (IV. vi. 207-8).

It is this complex resolution of feeling, issuing in new insight, that lies behind the use of 'nature' in *Macbeth*. Since the insight stems from a mode of being and is inseparable from it, it cannot be summed up in a formula. But in matters of this kind simple formulations have their uses, if only as a way of ensuring that necessary complexity has not, in the course of argument, degenerated into mere verbal complication, or that mountains are not being made out of molehills. Shakespeare, then, does not say that 'nature, however inscrutable, is basically beneficent'; he does not say that there is 'in nature a core of tenderness, which lies even deeper than pride or cruelty'[9]. He says—though it takes the whole of *King Lear* to say it adequately—that nature *per se* is something quite other than human nature, and that it cannot properly be conceived in human terms; that its humanly relevant quality only exists in relation to a particular human outlook and standpoint; and that what that quality is depends on the standpoint from which the relation is established. 'Nature-as-beneficent' is a concept that only has meaning for the good man—or at all events for the man who admits the imperatives of his own humanity. Perhaps it is easier to grasp this in relation to the world—the given 'nature'—of inner experience. The mind ('that ocean, where each kind Does straight its own resemblance find') contains within itself elements corresponding to non-human life—Blake's tiger and lamb. So long as these natural forces are not integrated by the specifically human principle they are, or are likely to become, chaotic and destructive. Given that principle, they may be sublimated and transformed, but they are not disowned: they are freely accepted as the natural sources of life and power[10]. So too with the external

world of nature: it is only the man who recognizes his own
humanity, and that of others, as something essentially
other than a product of the natural world, who is really
open to nature; neither fascinated nor afraid, he can
√ respond creatively to its creativeness, and, paradoxically,
find in nature a symbol for all that is natural in the other
√ sense—that is, most truly human. It is, I think, some such
perception as this, attained in *King Lear*, that lies behind
and validates the elaborate and imaginatively powerful
analogy between the human order and the order of
nature in *Macbeth*.

3

There is no vague 'philosophy of nature' in *Macbeth*.
The nature against which the 'unnaturalness' of the
Macbeth evil is defined and judged is human nature; and
essential characteristics of that nature—its capacity for
and intimate dependence on relationship—are powerfully
evoked throughout the play. In Act III, scene iv. Macbeth,
overcome by his vision of Banquo's ghost, glances back
to a time when murder was common, to what will later
be known as the Hobbesian state of nature.

> Blood hath been shed ere now, i' th' olden time,
> Ere humane statute purg'd the gentle weal;
> Ay, and since too, murthers have been perform'd
> Too terrible for the ear: the time has been,
> That, when the brains were out, the man would die,
> And there an end; but now, they rise again,
> With twenty mortal murthers on their crowns,
> And push us from our stools. This is more strange
> Than such a murther is.   (III. iv. 74-82)

This is a more profound version of the origins of society
than is suggested by the notion of contract or expediency.
What 'purges' the supposed mere multitude and makes
it into a 'gentle' commonweal is a decree greater than

any law in which it may be embodied, for it is what is dictated by the very fact of being human; if you accept your humanity then you can't murder with impunity. Nor is this simply a matter of judicial punishment: the murdered man 'rises' again, in you. Killing may be common in wild nature, but it is not natural to man as man; it is a violation of his essential humanity. When Lady Macbeth describes her husband as 'too full o'the milk of human kindness'[11] she intends to be disparaging, as Goneril does when she speaks of Albany's 'milky gentleness' or calls him a 'milk-liver'd man' (*King Lear*, I. iv. 351; IV. ii. 50). But what the phrase also says is that human kindness is natural to man as man, and, like his mother's milk, nourishes his manhood. When Malcolm accuses himself of imaginary crimes, and in so doing reflects the evil that Macbeth has brought on Scotland, the climax is,

> Nay, had I power, I should
> Pour the sweet milk of concord into Hell,
> Uproar the universal peace, confound
> All unity in earth. (IV. iii. 97-100)

'Concord', 'peace', 'unity'—these are *active* words, signifying not a mere absence of disagreeables, a mere deliverance from 'continual fear, and danger of violent death'[12], but the condition of positive human living. We learn little about a play by making lists of words, but it is a significant fact that *Macbeth* contains a very large number of words expressing the varied relations of life (not only 'cousin', 'children', 'servants', 'guest', 'host' . . ., but 'thanks', 'payment', 'service', 'loyalty', 'duties' . . .), and that these sometimes, as in Act I. scenes iv. and vi., seem to be dwelt on with a special insistence. At the end of the play, when Macbeth thinks of what he has lost, it is not 'honour, wealth and ease in waning age' (*Lucrece*, l. 142) but

that which should accompany old age,
As honour, love, obedience, troops of friends,

(v. iii. 24-5)

An awareness of those 'holy cords' which, though they
may be severed, are 'too intrince'—too intimately inter-
twined—'to unloose' (*King Lear*, II. ii. 75-6), is integral
to the imaginative structure of *Macbeth*. That the man
who breaks the bonds that tie him to other men, who
'pours the sweet milk of concord into Hell', is at the same
time violating his own nature and thwarting his own
deepest needs, is something that the play dwells on with
a special insistence.

Now as we have seen in relation to *King Lear* it is only
when the essential needs and characteristics of human
nature are given an absolute, unconditional priority, that
nature in its widest sense can be invoked as an order
underlying, invigorating, and in a certain sense offering a
pattern for, human nature. So too in *Macbeth*. In Macbeth's apocalyptic soliloquy before the murder, the 'Pity'
that dominates the chaotic natural forces and rides the
whirlwind appears as a new-born babe—an offspring of
humanity, naked, vulnerable, and powerful. It is, we
may say, because of the symbol of the babe, and all it
stands for, that Shakespeare can invoke the powers of
nature and associate them, as Professor Wilson Knight
shows that he does, with all that is opposed to, and finally
victorious over, the powers of destruction[13].

It is in the scene of Duncan's entry into Macbeth's
castle (I. vi.)—'a perfect contrast in microcosm to the
Macbeth evil'[14]—that we are most vividly aware of
the energies of untaught nature in significant relation to
the human order. The scene is set for full dramatic
effect between Lady Macbeth's invocation of the powers of
darkness ('The raven himself is hoarse, That croaks the
fatal entrance . . .') and Macbeth's final resolution, and

Duncan's courtesy underlines the irony. But the contrast is not confined to the situation. The suggestion of a sweet fresh air, the pleased contemplation of the birds that build and breed, affect us first as sensory contrasts to the smothering oppression ('Come, thick Night . . .') so recently evoked; but like the images of darkness and disorder the presented scene is inseparable from the values it embodies and defines.

> This guest of summer,
> The temple-haunting martlet, does approve,
> By his lov'd mansionry, that the heaven's breath
> Smells wooingly here: no jutty, frieze,
> Buttress, nor coign of vántage, but this bird
> Hath made his pendent bed, and procreant cradle:
> Where they most breed and haunt, I have observ'd
> The air is delicate.

What we are contemplating here is a natural and wholesome *order*, of which the equivalent in the human sphere is to be found in those mutualities of loyalty, trust and liking that Macbeth proposes to violate. And it is an order that is at one with the life it fosters. The opening lines of the scene, in short, are not only beautiful in themselves, they form an image of life delighting in life. It is in terms of destructive and self-destructive energies that Macbeth's power lust is defined; and it is from the 'life' images of the play, which range from the temple-haunting martlets to Macduff's 'babes', his 'pretty ones', and include all the scattered references to man's natural goods—sleep and food and fellowship—that we take our bearings in the apprehension of evil.

4

In the great soliloquy of I. vii. Macbeth tries to provide himself with prudential reasons for not committing murder:—

But in these cases,
We still have judgment here; that we but teach
Bloody instructions, which, being taught, return
To plague th'inventor.

But the attempt at a cool calculation of consequences (already at odds with the nervous rhythm and the taut muscular force of the imagery of the opening lines) almost immediately gives way to an appalling vision of judgment.

Besides, this Duncan
Hath borne his faculties so meek, hath been
So clear in his great office, that his virtues
Will plead like angels, trumpet-tongu'd, against
The deep damnation of his taking-off . . .

These lines have of course behind them the traditional conception of the Day of Judgment, and it is nothing less than the nature of judgment that the play reveals. Just as, in Spinoza's words 'blessedness is not the reward of virtue but virtue itself', so the deep damnation of this play is revealed in the intrinsic qualities of an evil deliberately willed and persisted in. It is revealed above all as a defection from life and reality.

So that in vent'ring ill we leave to be
The things we are for that which we expect;
And this ambitious foul infirmity,
In having much, torments us with defect
Of that we have: so then we do neglect
    The things we have, and, all for want of wit,
    Make something nothing by augmenting it.

So Shakespeare had written in *The Rape of Lucrece* (ll. 148-154), where lust—a type sin, 'including all foul harms' (l. 199)—was defined as the urge to possess something that in the experience inevitably proves mere loss, an over-reaching into insubstantiality and negation[15]. In *Macbeth* the positives so securely established—the assured intimation of 'the things we [*sc.* truly] are'—throw into relief, and so sharply define, the defection that occupies the forefront of the play. It is this that makes the play's irony so deeply significant—the irony of making 'something nothing by augmenting it', that is, in Banquo's phrase, 'by seeking to augment it' (II. i. 27); and that central irony of losing in gaining—for Macbeth, like Tarquin, is 'A captive victor that hath lost in gain' (*Lucrece*, l. 730)— lies behind all the often noted dramatic ironies that multiply as the play proceeds. Fear and disorder erupt into the specious security and apparent order that temporarily succeed the murder of Duncan[16]. 'Things bad begun' attempt to 'make strong themselves by ill', yet each further step is as 'tedious' (Macbeth's word) and self-frustrating as the last. And the concomitant of the outer disorder and inner disintegration (with both of which Macbeth identifies himself in the great invocation of chaos in IV. i.) is something that appears to the observer as the betrayal of life to automatism, and within Macbeth's own consciousness as a deepening sense of the loss of significance. It is a radical failure of the human to inhabit his proper world of creative activity. A brief examination of these two related aspects of that failure will conclude our examination of the play's philosophy.

We touch for the last time on the question of 'nature'. Early in the play we are told of 'the merciless Macdonwald' that he is 'worthy to be a rebel',

> for to that
> The multiplying villainies of nature
> Do swarm upon him. (I. ii. 9-12)

Now nature, we have seen, is a power that can be invoked in the service of what is essentially right and wholesome on the sole condition that 'human kindness' is recognized as an absolute. Nature by itself, however, is clearly a sub-moral world[17], and to 'Night's black agents' (III. ii. 53) in the outer world correspond, within,

> the cursed thoughts that nature
> Gives way to in repose.
>
> (II. i. 8-9)

Man, the inhabitant of two worlds, is free to choose; but if, disregarding the 'compunctious visitings of Nature', he chooses 'Nature's mischief' (I. v. 45, 50), his freedom is impaired. He has 'untied the winds' (IV. i. 52), and the powers of nature enter the human sphere as autonomous agents: in the language of the play, the 'villainies of nature' 'swarm upon him' as a more or less passive host[18].

The explanation of this phrase thus involves us in a consideration of one of the main structural lines of the play, where to the creative energy of good—enlisting and controlling nature's powers—is opposed the automatism of evil. To listen to the witches, it is suggested, is like eating 'the insane root, That takes the reason prisoner' (I. iii. 84-5); for Macbeth, in the moment of temptation, 'function', or intellectual activity, is 'smother'd in surmise'; and everywhere the imagery of darkness suggests not only the absence or withdrawal of light but—'light thickens'—the presence of something positively oppressive and impeding. Both Macbeth and his wife wilfully blind themselves ('Come, thick Night', 'Come, seeling Night . . .'), and to the extent that they surrender the characteristically human power of intellectual and moral discernment they themselves become the 'prey' of 'Night's black agents', of the powers they have deliberately invoked[19]. Automatism is perhaps most obvious in Lady Macbeth's sleep-walking, with its obsessed reliving of the past, but Macbeth also is shown as forfeiting his human freedom and spontaneity. If one

ultimate aspect of evil is revealed in Macbeth's invocation of chaos, in his determination to be answered,

> though the treasure
> Of Nature's germens tumble all together,
> Even till destruction sicken,

another is suggested by the banal repetitions of the
witches' incantations, the almost mechanical beat in
which their charms are 'wound up'. And just as the
widespreading confusion (enacted on the 'metaphy-
sical' plane) is reflected in the particular action, so Macbeth's terror-stricken advance in evil is tuned to that
monotonous beat. 'One feels', says W. C. Curry, 'that in
proportion as the good in him diminishes, his liberty of
free choice is determined more and more by evil inclination and that he cannot choose the better course. Hence
we speak of destiny or fate, as if it were some external
force or moral order, compelling him against his will to
certain destruction'[20]. Most readers have felt that after
the initial crime there is something compulsive in Macbeth's murders; and at the end, for all his 'valiant fury',
he is certainly not a free agent. He is like a bear tied to a
stake, he says; but it is not only the besieging army that
hems him in; he is imprisoned in the world he has made.

It is from within that world that, prompted by the
news of his wife's suicide, he speaks his last great speech.

> She should have died hereafter:
> There would have been a time for such a word.—
> To-morrow, and to-morrow, and to-morrow,
> Creeps in this petty pace from day to day,
> To the last syllable of recorded time;
> And all our yesterdays have lighted fools
> The way to dusty death. Out, out, brief candle!
> Life's but a walking shadow; a poor player,
> That struts and frets his hour upon the stage,

And then is heard no more: it is a tale
Told by an idiot, full of sound and fury,
Signifying nothing.

(v. v. 17-28)

His wife's death, it has often been observed, means nothing to him. Commentators have been exercised to determine the precise meaning of the words with which he greets it—'She should have died hereafter' ('She would have died sometime', or, 'Her death should have been deferred to a more peaceable hour'); but the point of the line lies in its ambiguity. Macbeth is groping for meanings, trying to conceive a time when he might have met such a situation with something more than indifference, when death itself might have had a significance it cannot have in the world of mere meaningless repetition that he goes on to evoke[21]. As a final irony this *is* the world where when a thing is done it is merely—'alms for oblivion'—done with, because it is a world devoid of significant relations.

Clearly then we have in this play an answer to Shakespeare's earlier questionings about time's power, as we have also a resolution of his earlier preoccupation with the power of illusion and false appearance. Macbeth *has betrayed himself* to the equivocal and the illusory. So too time appears to him as meaningless repetition because he has turned his back on, has indeed attempted violence on, those values that alone give significance to duration, that in a certain sense make time, for 'Without the meaning there is no time'[22]. He has directed his will to evil, towards something that of its very nature makes for chaos and the abnegation of meaning. The solid natural goods—ranging from food and sleep to the varied mutualities of friendship, service, love—are witnesses to the central paradox of evil, that however terrible its power it can only lead to 'nothing'.

141

In the lines,

> . . . it is a tale
> Told by an idiot, full of sound and fury,
> Signifying nothing,

there is combined the apparent force—the sound and
fury—and the essential meaninglessness. For Macbeth,
now, though in a different sense from when he used the
phrase, 'nothing is, but what is not'[23].

But the play's last word is not, of course, about evil.

> What's more to do,
> Which would be planted newly with the time,—
> As calling home our exil'd friends abroad,
> That fled the snares of watchful tyranny;
> Producing forth the cruel ministers
> Of this dead butcher, and his fiend-like Queen,
> Who, as 'tis thought, by self and violent hands
> Took off her life;—this, and what needful else
> That calls upon us, by the grace of Grace,
> We will perform in measure, time, and place.

It is a fitting close for a play in which moral law has been
made present to us not as convention or command
but as the law of life itself, as that which makes for life,
and through which alone man can ground himself on, and
therefore in his measure know, reality.

CHAPTER VII

Antony and Cleopatra and Coriolanus

I N both *Antony and Cleopatra* and *Coriolanus* we are confronted with something very different from the deliberate perversion of values that is the subject of *Macbeth*.
In each Shakespeare dramatizes modes of experience that
—for all the intensity with which they are expressed—we
recognize as coming very close indeed to the common run
of human experience. The themes of the two plays are
indeed complementary in obvious but interesting ways,
sexual passion being by its nature personal and subjective,
though never merely a matter of individual feeling, the
impulse towards authority and command necessarily
manifesting itself in a wide social field, though both its
origin and effects belong to the realm of personal life. In
each play, moreover, tragic failure is expressed in terms of
a failure of relationship between strongly asserted personal
values and something very much greater than those
values. And lest this should seem an intolerable moralizing
of poetry so commanding I would remind the reader of
two points that, I think, necessarily become clear in any
consistent attempt to follow the course of Shakespeare's
development. The first, already touched on, is that the
assured judgment of the later tragedies supervened on a
long process of personal questioning. Naturally I do not
mean that Shakespeare had to make his own standards:
it is obvious enough that he inherited a rich and complex
tradition of moral enquiry and evaluation. I mean that
because he had questioned experience with such urgent
honesty, the only answers that would serve were those
that satisfied the personality as a whole: Shakespeare's

judgment is not the application of a rule or measure, it is the bringing to bear of a sense of life as rich and generous as it is clear-eyed and not to be deceived. My second point, therefore, concerns the nature of moral judgment when this is equated with the imaginative apprehension of life working at its highest power. There is, as I have said, no question of the application of a formal code. When the imagination judges it does not hold at a distance; it brings close and makes vivid, and of any mode of being it asks only one question,—Does this, when most fully realized, when allowed to speak most clearly its own name, make for life?—life being understood not as random impulse but as power proceeding from an integrated personal centre, rational, clear-sighted and deeply responsive to all human claims. We touch here on what is only at first sight a paradox. It is because, in the later plays, judgment is made from a personal centre, in the light of values to which the whole personality gives its adherence, that it combines with so wide reaching a sympathy. In the last analysis perhaps we need not say that Shakespeare judges; he simply reveals.

I

In *Macbeth* we are never in any doubt of our moral bearings. *Antony and Cleopatra*, on the other hand, embodies different and apparently irreconcilable evaluations of the central experience. There is the view, with which the play opens, of those who stand outside the charmed circle of 'Egypt':

> Take but good note, and you shall see in him
> The triple pillar of the world transform'd
> Into a strumpet's fool.

(I. i. 11-13)

This attitude is strongly represented in the play; there are repeated references to 'lascivious wassails', 'the amorous

surfeiter', 'salt Cleopatra', 'the adulterous Antony' who
'gives his potent regiment to a trull', and so on. The
'Roman' world of war and government—the realm of
political 'necessity' (III. vi. 83) rather than of spontaneous
human feelings—is of course itself presented critically; but
although the way we take the Roman comments is partly
determined by our sense of the persons making them,
they do correspond to something of which we are directly
aware in the Egyptian scenes. We do not need any Roman
prompting to be aware of something cloying in the sexual
insistence (in the opening of I. ii, for example), and of
something practised in (to borrow a phrase from North)
the 'flickering enticements of Cleopatra unto Antonius'.

On the other hand, what Shakespeare infused into the
love story as he found it in Plutarch was an immense
energy, a sense of life so heightened that it can claim to
represent an absolute value:

> Eternity was in our lips, and eyes,
> Bliss in our brows' bent; none our parts so poor,
> But was a race of heaven.
>
> (I. iii. 35-7)

This energy communicates itself to all that comes within
the field of force that radiates from the lovers, and within
which their relationship is defined. In Enobarbus's description of the first meeting of Antony and Cleopatra (II. ii.
190 ff.) the energy counteracts the suggestion of a deliberate sensuousness; the inanimate is felt as animate; and
the passage, although a set-piece, modulates easily into a
racy buoyancy:

> The city cast
> Her people out upon her; and Antony,
> Enthron'd i' the market-place, did sit alone,
> Whistling to the air; which, but for vacancy,
> Had gone to gaze on Cleopatra too,
> And make a gap in nature.

Wilson Knight rightly insists on 'the impregnating atmosphere of wealth, power, military strength and material magnificence', the cosmic imagery, and 'the continual suggestion of earth's fruitfulness', in terms of which Antony and Cleopatra are presented to us[1], and the suggestions of scope and grandeur are blended with continual reminders of what is common to humanity. It is the richness and energy of the poetry in which all this is conveyed that, more than any explicit comment, defines for us the vitality of the theme.

Shakespeare, in short, evokes the passion of the lovers with the greatest possible intensity, and invests it with the maximum of positive significance. But, more realist than some of his critics, he makes it impossible for us not to question the nature and conditions of that very energy that the lovers release in each other. The sequence of scenes between Actium and the final defeat of Antony opens, as Granville-Barker noticed[2], with a suggestion of dry and brittle comedy. In an apparent abeyance of feeling the lovers are more or less pushed into each other's arms by their respective followers; and there is an inert resignation in the reconciliation that follows. Here indeed the most memorable verse is not love poetry at all; it is Antony's bare and emphatic statement,

> Egypt, thou knew'st too well,
> My heart was to thy rudder tied by the strings,
> And thou shouldst tow me after. O'er my spirit
> Thy full supremacy thou knew'st, and that
> Thy beck might from the bidding of the gods
> Command me.

> (III. xi. 56-61)

Feeling does not well up in Antony until he discovers Caesar's messenger kiss:ng Cleopatra's hand. It is a perverse violence of cruelty—'Whip him, fellows, Till like a

146

boy you see him cringe his face'—that goads him into a semblance of energy; and it is in the backwash of this emotion that Cleopatra can humour him until she is, as it were, again present to him. Shakespeare, however, leaves us in no doubt about the overwrought nature of Antony's feelings: the very look of him is given us by Enobarbus— 'Now he'll outstare the lightning' (III. xiii. 195).

Antony, in short, is galvanized into feeling; there is no true access of life and energy. And the significance of this is that we know that what we have to do with is an emphatic variation of a familiar pattern. Looking back, we can recall how often this love has seemed to thrive on emotional stimulants. They were necessary for much the same reason as the feasts and wine. For the continued references to feasting—and it is not only Caesar and his dry Romans who emphasize the Alexandrian consumption of food and drink—are not simply a means of intensifying the imagery of tasting and savouring that is a constant accompaniment of the love theme; they serve to bring out the element of repetition and monotony in a passion which, centring on itself, is self-consuming, leading ultimately to what Antony himself, in a most pregnant phrase, names as 'the heart of loss'. Indeed, the speech in which this phrase occurs (IV. xii. 9-30) is one of the pivotal things in the play. In its evocation of an appalled sense of insubstantiality it ranks with Macbeth's, 'My thought, whose murder yet is but fantastical . . .' With this difference: that whereas Macbeth is, as it were, reaching forward to a region 'where nothing is, but what is not', Antony is driven to recognize the element of unreality and enchantment in what he had thought was solid and enduring. The speech has a superb sensuous reality that is simultaneously felt as discandying or melting, until the curious flicker of the double vision—both intensified and explained by the recurrent theme of

147

'Egyptian' magic and gipsy-like double-dealing—is resolved in the naked vision:

> O sun, thy uprise shall I see no more,
> Fortune and Antony part here, even here
> Do we shake hands. All come to this? The hearts
> That spaniel'd me at heels, to whom I gave
> Their wishes, do discandy, melt their sweets
> On blossoming Caesar: and this pine is bark'd
> That overtopp'd them all. Betray'd I am.
> O this false soul of Egypt! this grave charm,
> Whose eye beck'd forth my wars, and call'd them
>   home;
> Whose bosom was my crownet, my chief end,
> Like a right gipsy, hath at fast and loose
> Beguil'd me, to the very heart of loss.[3]
>
> (IV. xii. 18-29)

Cleopatra's lament over the dying Antony, her evocation of his greatness and bounty, have perhaps weighed too heavily in the impression that many people have taken from the play as a whole. That these things are great poetry goes without saying. But the almost unbearable pathos of the last scenes is for what has not in fact been realized[4].

> CLEOPATRA.   For his bounty,
>   There was no winter in't: an autumn 'twas
>   That grew the more by reaping: his delights
>   Were dolphin-like, they show'd his back above
>   The element they lived in: in his livery
>   Walk'd crowns and crownets: realms and islands
>   were
>   As plates dropp'd from his pocket.
> DOLABELLA.   Cleopatra!
> CLEOPATRA. Think you there was, or might be such a
>   man
>   As this I dreamt of?

148

DOLABELLA. Gentle madam, no.
CLEOPATRA. You lie up to the hearing of the gods.
But if there be, nor ever were one such,
It's past the size of dreaming: nature wants stuff
To vie strange forms with fancy, yet to imagine
An Antony were nature's piece 'gainst fancy,
Condemning shadows quite.

(v. ii. 86-100)

The figure that Cleopatra evokes may not be fancy—the poetry invests it with a substantial reality; but it is not the Antony that the play has given us; it is something disengaged from, or glimpsed through, that Antony. Nor should the power and beauty of Cleopatra's last great speech obscure the continued presence of something self-deceiving and unreal. She may speak of the baby at her breast that sucks the nurse asleep; but it is not, after all, a baby—new life; it is simply death.

It is, of course, one of the signs of a great writer that he can afford to evoke sympathy or even admiration for what, in his final judgment, is discarded or condemned. In *Antony and Cleopatra* the sense of potentiality in life's untutored energies is pushed to its limit, and Shakespeare gives the maximum weight to an experience that is finally 'placed'. It is perhaps this that makes the tragedy so sombre in its realism, so little comforting to the romantic imagination. For Shakespeare has chosen as his tragic theme the impulse that man perhaps most readily associates with a heightened sense of life and fulfilment. It has not seemed necessary here to explore the range and depth of the poetry in which the theme of vitality twinned with frustration, of force that entangles itself with strength, is expressed; but it is, of course, the range and depth of the poetry that make Antony and Cleopatra into universal figures. At the superb close, Cleopatra—both 'empress' and 'lass unparallel'd'—is an incarnation of sexual passion,

of those primeval energies that insistently demand fulfilment in their own terms, and, by insisting on their own
terms ('Thy beck might from the bidding of the gods
Command me'), thwart the fulfilment that they seek.
'There is no evil impulse', says Martin Buber, 'till the
impulse has been separated from the being'[5]. It is
precisely this that *The Tragedy of Antony and Cleopatra*
reveals.

2

Shakespeare's earlier plays on political themes, from
Henry VI onwards, had shown an increasing realism, a
developing concern for the actuality—the specific human
substance—of situations commonly seen in abstract and
general terms. *Coriolanus*, in this respect, is the consum-
mation of Shakespeare's political wisdom. But if *Coriolanus*
thus links with a large group of earlier plays, it could only
have been written after *King Lear* and *Macbeth*. There is
now an assured grasp of those positive values that alone
give significance to conflict; the play is a tragedy, not a
satire. And the verse, close packed and flexible, has that
power of compressed definition that we associate with the
plays of Shakespeare's maturity, so that the immediate
action is felt as the focus of a vision of life that is searching
and profound.

Caius Marcius dominates the action of the play to which
he gives his name, but the protagonist is Rome, the
city[6]. It is a city divided against itself, and the first
scene presents the conflict in lively, dramatic terms. It
also contains Menenius's fable of the belly, which is a
reminder of the ideal of mutuality in a healthy social
organism, but which certainly does not answer the specific complaints of the citizens—'What authority surfeits
on would relieve us'. Menenius himself habitually thinks
in terms of a distinction between 'Rome' and 'her rats';

and although there is no idealization of 'the people'—
who are a mixed assortment of individuals—the courtesy
of the patrician class among themselves is more than once
placed in effective contrast to their rudeness to the
plebeians[7]. A semblance of unity is restored by the
granting of tribunes to the plebs and by the approach of
external danger. The battle scenes show us the real bravery
of Caius Marcius, as well as the less admirable characteristics of some of the commoners. They also make us
vividly aware of the simplifying effect of war; but with
the return of peace internal strain promptly reasserts
itself. Coriolanus's behaviour in seeking the consulship
brings the conflict to a head.

No summary account can do justice to the dramatic
and poetic force of the third act which culminates in
Coriolanus's banishment, but three points may be mentioned. The first is that in such things as Coriolanus's
speech at III. i. 139-60, we are vividly aware of the social
conflict as a conflict of vital energies that have become
inextricably tangled in a process of mutual thwarting and
stultification:

> . . . purpose so barr'd, it follows
> Nothing is done to purpose.

Secondly, a large part of the meaning is conveyed by a
sharp intensification of the imagery of disease; what each
side wants is health or 'integrity', but each can think only
in terms of surgery, of 'plucking out' a tongue (III. i.
154-5), or 'cutting away' a diseased limb (III. i. 292). And
in the third place, when we relate this superb act to the
play as a whole, it is impossible not to connect the
'disease' of the body politic with the lop-sided development, the defective humanity, of the central figure.

The fact that our sense of Coriolanus is created largely
by poetic means[8] should not hinder us from seeing in

the play a subtle psychological probing of the springs of conduct, or a rich sociological interest. When, in the first scene of the play, Coriolanus's prowess is mentioned, we are told, 'He did it to please his mother, and to be partly proud' (I. i. 37-8). Almost immediately after the first public appearance of the hero, we are given a domestic scene in which our attention is directed to the mother, and the mother as a representative of a class (the very tones of 'polite' conversation are caught in the Lady Valeria). Volumnia, the Roman matron, is a perfect embodiment of what has been called 'the taboo on tenderness' [9]. The culture of which she is a representative stresses those 'masculine' qualities that range from genuine physical courage to hardness and insensitiveness in the face of life: her laconic comment on young Marcius's 'mammocking' of the butterfly—'One on's father's moods'—is worth several pages of analysis. Now in the great central scenes the patrician 'honour' to which she so frequently appeals is subjected to a radical scrutiny. Act III, scene ii, shows the patricians in council after Coriolanus's first reverse; the question is whether he shall submit himself to the people, and Volumnia urges a politic submission:

> . . . now it lies you on to speak
> To the people; not by your own instruction,
> Nor by the matter which your heart prompts you,
> But with such words that are but roted in
> Your tongue, though but bastards and syllables
> Of no allowance to your bosom's truth.
> Now, this no more dishonours you at all
> Than to take in a town with gentle words,
> Which else would put you to your fortune and
> The hazard of much blood.
> I would dissemble with my nature where
> My fortunes and my friends at stake requir'd
> I should do so in honour.

(III. ii. 53-64)

It is to the spirit of this that Coriolanus finally responds:

Pray, be content:
Mother, I am going to the market-place;
Chide me no more. I'll mountebank their loves,
Cog their hearts from them, and come home belov'd
Of all the trades in Rome.

(III. ii. 130-4)

I do not remember seeing it remarked in any commentary on the play that the 'honour' in question, being divorced from the 'bosom's truth', is of a very dubious quality, and that Coriolanus, in agreeing to this persuasion, shows a wanton disregard for the values that form the moral basis of any decent society, just as they are at the heart of personal relationships:

I'll mountebank their loves,
Cog their hearts from them . . .

Coriolanus has none of the apocalyptic quality of *Macbeth*. It is not a world where the sun refuses to rise or horses eat each other; it is a world where petty justices 'wear out a good wholesome forenoon in hearing a cause between an orange-wife and a forset-seller', where people 'buy and sell with groats', and 'tradesmen sing in their shops'—a familiar world; yet the evil at the heart of the state—though not, as in *Macbeth*, deliberately willed—is just as firmly stated as in the earlier tragedy. In cutting himself off from a responsive relationship to his society (as he had in fact already done before his banishment) Coriolanus has diminished his own stature as a human being[10]:

—I go alone,
Like to a lonely dragon, that his fen
Makes fear'd and talk'd of more than seen.

(IV. i. 29-31)

And in the concluding acts there are constant reminders of the unnatural reversal of values in social life that springs

from a personal failure to achieve integration and relationship. Thus the 'comic' talk of the serving-men (IV. v)
about the superiority of war to peace (peace 'makes men
hate one another'—'Reason: because they then less need
one another') merely transposes into another key Volumnia's denial of values essential to life. The logic of that
denial, which her son accepts, is worked out to its end;
and the imagery of falling and burning buildings in the
latter part of the play suggests the public counterpart to
the angry isolation and self-destruction of one who, being
a man, can only find his true life in society:

> I'll never
> Be such a gosling to obey instinct, but stand
> As if a man were author of himself,
> And knew no other kin.

(v. iii. 34-7)

In the face of his mother's dignified and moving appeal
to spare the city, Coriolanus finds that he has to 'obey
instinct', and there is tragic dignity in his reply to
Volumnia:

> O, mother, mother!
> What have you done? Behold the heavens do ope,
> The gods look down, and this unnatural scene
> They laugh at. O my mother, mother! O!
> You have won a happy victory to Rome;
> But, for your son, believe it, O, believe it,
> Most dangerously you have with him prevail'd,
> If not most mortal to him. But let it come.

(v. iv. 182-9)

But there is also tragic irony; it is to his mother that he
yields—the mother who has made him what he is. He
returns to Antium, 'No more infected with my country's
love Than when I parted thence' (v. vi. 71-2), still unable
to know, to recognize, 'the other kin', who would
include even the plebeians, with their 'pardons, being

asked, as free As words to little purpose' (III. ii. 88-9). At
the height of the civil commotion, we may recall,
Cominius had attempted to intervene:

> Let me speak:
> I have been consul, and can show for Rome
> Her enemies' marks upon me. I do love
> My country's good with a respect more tender,
> More holy and profound, than mine own life,
> My dear wife's estimate, her womb's increase
> And treasure of my loins.
>
> (III. iii. 109-15)

There is suggested the reconciling conception of the state
as an extension of the organic bonds of the family, a
conception analogous to the ideal of creative mutuality
hinted at by Menenius's fable of the belly. But a whole-
hearted response to that ideal demands some personal
integration and maturity, and Coriolanus, as Wyndham
Lewis remarked[11], remains to the end the 'boy' that
Aufidius taunts him with being.

Not indeed that we accept Aufidius's perverse statement of the whole situation.

> You lords and heads o'the state, perfidiously
> He has betray'd your business, and given up,
> For certain drops of salt, your city Rome,
> I say 'your city', to his wife and mother;
> Breaking his oath and resolution like
> A twist of rotten silk, never admitting
> Counsel o' the war; but at his nurse's tears
> He whin'd and roar'd away your victory,
> That pages blush'd at him, and men of heart
> Look'd wondering each at other.
>
> (v. vi. 90-9)

That, taken as a whole, is a lie. But as defence against it
Coriolanus can only reassert those partial and over-sim-
plified values which, accepted as absolutes, have stood

between him and an adequately integrated and responsive life. That is his personal tragedy. But there is also the tragedy of the divided and mutilated city; and a fundamental insight that this play embodies is that political and social forms cannot be separated from, are in fact judged by, the human and moral qualities that shape them, and the human and moral qualities that they foster. That is Shakespeare's answer to Renaissance and modern 'realism' that would resolve political questions solely to questions of power. There are wide implications here that may perhaps be suggested by the compressed and powerful lines from Blake's *Jerusalem*—

> The land is mark'd for desolation & unless we plant
> The seeds of Cities & of Villages in the Human
> bosom
> Albion must be a rock of blood.[12]

Conclusion

THE argument of this extended essay—which obviously makes no pretence to inclusiveness or finality—is, I trust, sufficiently clear. What I have tried to suggest is a point of view from which Shakespeare's plays can be seen as related parts of a continuous exploration of the reality that is common to all men. Coleridge, it is well known, believing that 'no man was ever yet a great poet, without being at the same time a profound philosopher', claimed that Shakespeare was 'the guide and the pioneer of true philosophy'. It is a large claim, for clearly Shakespeare is not a philosophic poet in the sense in which Dante or Milton is a philosophic poet. Yet 'philosophic', meaning more than merely meditative or thoughtful, is a word one can hardly avoid in attempting to describe essential aspects of his genius. Professor Virgil Whitaker, in his suggestive book on Shakespeare's use of contemporary learning and ideas, finds it necessary to issue a warning. 'I know very well,' he says, 'that Shakespeare was writing plays and not philosophic treatises and that character and action were more important to him than abstract ideas. . . . Shakespeare used ideas to interpret character and action.' True; but it would be equally true to say that Shakespeare used the analysis of character and personality in the exploration of ideas: the ideas in question being not 'abstract ideas' but themes and preoccupations of great personal urgency, which demanded to be worked out not logically and in abstraction but in terms of the greatest possible exposure to life and the imaginative apprehension of it. Leone Vivante says of all true poets:

The strength of their words lies above all in a deepening realization of the spirit. I maintain that all literary value is also a philosophic achievement; that there is no trace of beauty which is not a reflection— and a discovery—of the intrinsic nature of inner being.

It is the strength, integrity and coherence of Shakespeare's exploration of the intrinsic nature of inner being, the strength, integrity and coherence of his *poetic thought*, that makes his work something properly described as a philosophic achievement, though of a kind that could only be made by a poet. He is concerned not with speculation about the ultimate nature of things, the relation of mind to matter, and so on, but with the question of value as it can be known and embodied under the conditions of life as we know it.

From this point of view, *King Lear* is the great central masterpiece, the great exploratory allegory to which so many of the earlier plays lead and on which the later plays depend. Those written before *Lear* stand firmly enough in their own right, but behind some of the most significant of them there is an insistent and unresolved questioning. It is implied in the measured declamation of Agamemnon:

> The ample proposition that hope makes
> In all designs begun on earth below
> Fails in the promis'd largeness: checks and disasters
> Grow in the veins of actions highest rear'd . . .

Why do both the public world and the world of intense subjective experience seem somehow flawed and unsatisfactory? Is there any escape from appearance and illusion? What is the status of human values in a world dominated by time and death? On what, in the world as we know it, can man take his stand? In *King Lear* Shakespeare discovered an answer to these questions not in terms of copy-book maxims but in terms of intense living experience. The resulting freedom from inner tensions is seen alike in the assured judgment and the magnificent vitality of *Macbeth*, *Antony and Cleopatra* and *Coriolanus*, in each of which qualities making for wholeness and essential life are glimpsed through the perversion or entanglement of energies and passions deeply rooted in human nature. In the latest plays, without discarding or ignoring the experience of the tragic period, Shakespeare puts in the forefront of his drama 'the possible other case', and directly bodies forth experiences in which not only does good triumph but the energies of 'nature' themselves contribute to the sense of renewed life[1].

Notes

1. Henri Fluchère, *Shakespeare* (translated by Guy Hamilton), p. 204.
2. Christopher Morris, *Political Thought in England: Tyndale to Hooker* (H.U.L.), p. x.

1. 'It is suggested, then, that a dramatic poet cannot create characters of the greatest intensity of life unless his personages, in their reciprocal actions and behaviour in their story, are somehow dramatizing, but in no obvious form, an action or struggle for harmony in the soul of the poet.' I suppose that this, from T. S. Eliot's essay on John Ford— *Selected Essays* (1932), p. 196—would now be generally accepted. It is in this essay that Mr Eliot speaks of the different works of a great poet as 'united by one significant, consistent, and developing personality' (p. 203).

2. By John Holloway, for example, in his broadcast talks on 'The New "Establishment" in Criticism', *The Listener*, September 20th and 27th, 1956.
   Arthur Sewell's *Character and Society in Shakespeare* is the most useful account known to me of the meanings of the term, 'character', as applied to Shakespeare's poetic drama.

3. In *Joseph Quincy Adams: Memorial Studies*, ed. J. G. McManaway and others (The Folger Shakespeare Library, 1948), pp. 81 ff.

4. It is of course true, as Professor Campbell contends, that Shakespeare did not give 'an arbitrary symbolical value' to certain words; nor did he 'manipulate' his imagery in a 'consciously scheming fashion'. Since I have quoted from this essay for my own purposes it is only fair to add that its intention—to insist that Shakespeare's 'comprehensiveness and complexity' should not be racked to fit a preconceived scheme—is entirely laudable.

5. Dr Tillyard says: ' "contagious" (suggesting sickness) and the sun combine to indicate the King's present sickness through poison'

NOTES

(Shakespeare's History Plays, p. 219). If I disagree with this it is for the reasons indicated in the remainder of the paragraph.

6. W. Empson has some other interesting suggestions concerning the uncanny 'atmosphere' of these lines. See *Seven Types of Ambiguity* (1930), pp. 23-5.

7. The reference to Chapter XV of the *Biographia Literaria* is deliberate.

8. Note for *At the Hawk's Well*.

9. Sir John Davies, Epigram 17.

10. A useful short summary is given by Bertram Joseph in the chapter, 'The Elizabethan Stage and Acting'—*A Guide to English Literature*, 2, *The Age of Shakespeare*, edited by Boris Ford, pp. 147 ff.

11. In 'Tragedy and the "Medium"' in *The Common Pursuit*, F. R. Leavis has some admirably suggestive comments on the nature of what he calls 'exploratory creation'.

12. See Lascelles Abercrombie's British Academy Lecture (1930), 'A Plea for the Liberty of Interpreting', included in *Aspects of Shakespeare;* also my essay 'On Historical Scholarship and the Interpretation of Shakespeare', *The Sewanee Review*, LXIII, 2 (1955), and Professor J. J. Lawlor's rejoinder in the same journal, LXIV, 2 (1956).

CHAPTER II

1. 'Shakespeare in his first tragedy, *Titus Andronicus*, imitated Seneca; in his first comedy, *The Comedy of Errors*, Plautus; and in his first poem, *Venus and Adonis*, Ovid.'—Peter Alexander, *Shakespeare's Life and Art*, pp. 58-9. '*The Comedy of Errors* and *Titus Andronicus* revealed their author as ambitious. If he wrote *1 Henry VI* about the same time, the extent of his ambitions is enlarged. Here we have a young man trying his hand in three great literary modes, classical comedy, Senecan tragedy, and, in keeping with the political proclivities of his age, a highly serious historical play. We find, not the brilliant apprentice and tinker of others' matter but an original poet, educated, confident of himself, already dedicated to poetry; a man passing through the states common to any very great artist, akin to Dante and Milton not only through mature achievement but in the manner in which he began his life-work.'—E. M. W. Tillyard, *Shakespeare's History Plays*, p. 141.

2. I have developed this theme in an Inaugural Lecture, *Poetry, Politics and the English Tradition*, and in 'Shakespeare's Politics; with Some

Reflections on the Nature of 'Tradition', the Annual Shakespeare Lecture of the British Academy, 1957. As Mr Patrick Cruttwell says in *The Shakespearean Moment* (p. 31), 'Politics, for [Shakespeare], meant the behaviour of individuals. Between the fields of politics, morals and psychology, he, like his age, made no clear divisions.' See also John Palmer, *The Political Characters of Shakespeare*.

3. See E. M. W. Tillyard's *Shakespeare's History Plays*, and A. P. Rossiter's Preface to the anonymous *Woodstock* (*Woodstock, a Moral History*).

4. Shakespeare's scene is in the spirit of Sir Thomas More's account of the same event in *The History of King Richard III:*—'And in a stage play all the people know right well that he that playeth the Sultan is percase a souter [shoemaker]. Yet if one should can so little good, to show out of season what acquaintance he hath with him, and call him by his own name while he standeth in his majesty, one of his tormentors (*i.e.* the stage tyrant's *tortores*) might hap to break his head, and worthy, for marring of the play. And so they (the citizens) said that these matters be King's games, as it were stage plays, and for the more part played upon scaffolds. In which poor men be but the lookers-on. And they that be wise will meddle no further. For they that sometimes step up and play with them, when they cannot play their parts, they disorder the play and do themselves no good.'— *The English Works of Sir Thomas More*, Vol. I, edited by W. E. Campbell, pp. 447-8.

5. Derek Traversi, 'Shakespeare: the Young Dramatist', in *A Guide to English Literature; the Age of Shakespeare*, edited by Boris Ford (Pelican Books), pp. 181-2. Mr Traversi, whose essay contains many pertinent observations on the earlier plays, adds: 'The creation of character, indeed, is not to be regarded as the unique, or even principal, end of Shakespeare's dramatic creations, in which plot and character, themselves handled with greater flexibility and insight, tend increasingly to find their proper context in a more ample artistic unity which embraces and illuminates them; but in the delineation of motive beyond the limits of convention his language first attained some sense of its full possibilities.'

6. See Grace Stuart, *Narcissus: a Psychological Study of Self Love*, pp. 81, 129.

7. See R. W. Chambers, *Thomas More*, p. 117.

8. *3 Henry VI*, v. vi. Richard had already expressed himself to similar effect in the long soliloquy in III. ii.

Why, love forswore me in my mother's womb . . .
And am I then a man to be beloved? . . .
Then, since this earth affords no joy to me,
But to command, to check, to o'erbear such
As are of better person than myself,
I'll make my heaven to dream upon the crown.

9. *Shakespeare's Doctrine of Nature: a Study of 'King Lear,'* pp. 58 ff.

10. *Poetry, Politics and the English Tradition,* p. 15.
The method in the passage on 'worshipful society' is not unlike that of Burns in, say, 'The Twa Dogs'.

> Or maybe in a frolic daft,
> To Hague or Calais takes a waft,
> To make a tour an' tak a whirl,
> To learn *bon ton* an' see the worl'.
>
> There, at Vienna or Versailles,
> He rives his father's auld entails;
> Or by Madrid he takes the rout,
> To thrum guitars an' fecht wi' nowt.

Mr John Speirs, in his brilliant essay on Burns in *The Scots Literary Tradition,* comments on the way in which the world of the fashionable tour suffers satiric depreciation merely by being 'balanced against the more immediate "local" world' present in the vocabulary and idiom.

11. The plays, of course, are not freely devised for the dramatist's particular purposes. Historical matter taken over from the chroniclers (as later from Plutarch) set limits and—to some extent—determined direction. But in art material is not simply 'taken over'; it only exists as treated; and it seems clear that Shakespeare used his historical données not simply to represent 'what happened' but to focus questions that interested him.

12. By the Bishop of Carlisle,

> Peace shall go sleep with Turks and infidels,
> And in this seat of peace tumultuous wars
> Shall kin with kin and kind with kind confound . . .
> O, if you raise this house against this house,
> It will the woefullest division prove
> That ever fell upon this cursed earth . . .

(IV. i. 139-47)

and by Richard himself (addressing Northumberland),

> The time shall not be many hours of age
> More than it is, ere foul sin gathering head
> Shall break into corruption: thou shalt think,
> Though he divide the realm, and give thee half,
> It is too little, helping him to all;
> And he shall think that thou, which know'st the way
> To plant unrightful kings, wilt know again,
> Being ne'er so little urged, another way
> To pluck him headlong from the usurped throne.
> The love of wicked men converts to fear;
> That fear to hate, and hate turns one or both
> To worthy danger and deserved death.

(v. i. 57-68)

13. Middleton Murry, 'The Creation of Falstaff', in *Discoveries*.

CHAPTER III

1. There are of course others notable as poetry that do nor fall within this grouping. Of these some are interesting for the introduction of new tones, notably of a detached irony: I should instance especially some of the 'rival poet' group—LXXIX to LXXXVII, for example. Others again express bitterness, protest and self-accusation, with a vigour of phrasing and rhythm which, if it does not always fully define the painful feelings involved, is a clear sign of the breaking through of new insights.

2. That these three bits of observation are recklessly thrown into the passing jest of a satirical knave (*Troilus and Cressida*, iii. iii.) suggests something of the unfailing Shakespearean abundance.

3. In a book on *The Elizabethan Love Sonnet* that appeared after this chapter was drafted, Mr J. W. Lever has put forward a well argued case (pp. 162-272) for finding in Shakespeare's Sonnets a significant development, culminating in a genuine resolution of conflicts springing from a deeply experienced sense of the precariousness of human values in a world where man's faults and Time's power are inescapable facts. A passionate friendship—in which the Friend is the epitome of beauty and truth, and the Poet's love for him 'the crystallization, in terms of a personal medium, of the artist's love of life on all the planes of phenomenal being' (p. 187)—is torn apart by faults on both sides, and the ideal qualities glimpsed in the Friend are exposed as

subject to time and change. It is because the facts are so honestly recognized that the poet is able to disengage from all the relativities of everyday living the one absolute of human experience, which is the transforming power of love. In the sonnets that Mr Lever sees as concluding the series a deliberate survey of the worst that Time can do (e.g. Sonnet LX) leads into a triumphant affirmation of a love which is not subject to his power (Sonnets CXV, CXXIV, CXXV, CXVI, CVII, LV).

Mr Lever's chapter contains some of the most intelligent criticism of the Sonnets that I have seen, and all readers of Shakespeare can learn from it: notably from his insistence on the way in which the Sonnets are permeated with the great central concerns of the age (cf. pp. 166-167 and p. 276), from his description of the quasi-dramatic function of the imagery (p. 168), from his account of the influence—both pervasive and specific—of the last Book of Ovid's *Metamorphoses* (pp. 248-72 *passim*), and from some brilliant particular analysis; and even those who do not completely accept his re-ordering of the sequence are likely to agree that he has brought together many sonnets that are mutually illuminating. But after much pondering I still feel that the affirmation of love's power—which for Mr Lever is a triumphant and grounded assertion of a lived experience—is to some extent *anticipatory*. Mr Lever's case, in short, depends on attributing to certain sonnets a depth and range of significance that I cannot find there. His account of Sonnet LX, Like as the waves make towards the pebbled shore' (pp. 252-5) is sensitive criticism of a kind that makes my own comments on that poem seem very inadequate indeed; yet even here, it seems to me, the argument is pushed too hard.

> Nativity, once in the main of light,
> Crawls to maturity, wherewith being crown'd,
> Crooked eclipses 'gainst his glory fight,
> And Time that gave doth now his gift confound.

Here is indeed 'a compound universal metaphor', and Mr Lever convincingly demonstrates how wide-reaching it is; yet to speak of the first three lines of the quatrain as 'an epitome . . . of all Shakespearean tragedies' is, surely, to read into them more than they will bear. Similarly, Sonnet CVII ('Not mine own fears, nor the prophetic soul of the wide world') is said to commemorate 'a moment of stillness when all the contradictions of life are suspended in the autumn glow of Love's victory over Time' (p. 267). That, no doubt, is the claim made by the poem itself; but we may still question the justice of the claim:

Now with the drops of this most balmy time
My love looks fresh, and Death to me subscribes . . .

Death as it is felt in *Hamlet?* or as when Lear enters with Cordelia dead in his arms? I still feel, in short, that the defiance of Time, though real enough and certainly indicative of the *direction* of growth, cannot be effective until the challenge of negation has been faced more fully and the resolution worked out at even deeper levels. Indeed in *Lear* and the later plays there is no defiance, and the fundamental acceptance of life that they embody is the more assured because, subjected to a keener testing, it takes up into itself doubts and questionings that are all but overwhelming. But *anticipation* of what is still to come there certainly is in the Sonnets (indeed the final resolution might well be described in the strange phrase of Sonnet CVII, 'Incertainties now crown themselves assur'd'), and Mr Lever's account should be read by all who are interested in the nature and direction of the experience that they embody.

4. In each instance Shakespeare is drawing on the passage from Book XV of Ovid's *Metamorphoses* which so haunted his imagination. See Knox Pooler's Arden edition of the Sonnets, p. 66, and, more especially, J. W. Lever, *The Elizabethan Love Sonnet*, pp. 248 ff.

5. The Scriptural references in which both parts of this play abound (see Richmond Noble, *Shakespeare's Biblical Knowledge*, pp. 169-81) seem to me to take on a more severe significance in Part II; in the scene under consideration the references to Job, in particular—'and your bodies like the clay' (xiii. 12), 'his candle shall be put out with him' (xviii. 6), and 'Among old persons there is wisdom, and in age is understanding' (xii. 12)—seem to point a sombre irony. Noble (p. 65 and p. 174) says that 2 *Henry IV* 'is the earliest play in which Genevan readings show a decided preponderance over Bishops'', which suggests a comparatively fresh re-reading of considerable parts of the Bible at this time.

6. The very slight alteration of the Folio punctuation that I have made here seems to me to give excellent sense to a passage usually labelled corrupt. Lord Bardolph says, in effect, 'Yes, it does do harm, if (as in the present case) a military enterprise relies on hope prematurely aroused, as when we see buds appear in a too early spring etc. The line 'Indeed the instant action, a cause on foot,' is emphatic repetition as Bardolph tries to impress Hastings with his own sense of the desperate importance of seeing their present enterprise as an example of the general rule about not counting your chickens, etc.

NOTES

7. Dr Tillyard (*Shakespeare's History Plays*, p. 303) aptly quotes Hardy's 'In a Time of the Breaking of Nations'.

8. 'By my troth, I care not; a man can die but once: we owe God a death: I'll ne'er bear a base mind: an't be my destiny, so; an't be not, so: no man's too good to serve his prince; and let it go which way it will, he that dies this year is quit for the next' (III. ii. 230-4).

9. See Leslie Hotson's essay, 'Ancient Pistol', in *Shakespeare's Sonnets Dated and Other Essays*.

10. 'If the young dace be a bate for the old pike, I see no reason in the law of nature but I may snap at him [Shallow]' (III. ii. 325-7).

11. *Scrutiny*, XV, 2, Spring, 1948. This essay is incorporated in Mr Traversi's *Shakespeare from 'Richard II' to 'Henry V'* (1957).

12. IV. i. 70-3 (Vaughan's 'shore'—Folio, 'there'—is adopted by Professor Dover Wilson in the New Cambridge edition), IV. ii. 33-5. Both these passages are spoken by the Archbishop of York. Bolingbroke's version of affairs is similar: he had no intention of taking the throne from Richard, 'But that necessity so bow'd the state, That I and greatness were compell'd to kiss' (III. ii. 73-4); and of the rebellion against himself, 'Are these things then necessities? Then let us meet them like necessities' (III. i. 92-3).

13.   [Love] fears not policy, that heretic,
        Which works on leases of short-number'd hours . . .
        (Sonnet CXXIV)

14. There are the obvious parallels—*King Lear*, IV. ii. 29-50, *Macbeth*, IV. i. 50-60; also of course *Sir Thomas More*, II. iv. and *Troilus and Cressida*, I. iii. 108-24. Of the passage quoted in the text Professor Dover Wilson aptly asks, 'What does not Pope's famous conclusion to *The Dunciad* owe to it?'

15. See D. A. Traversi's essay already referred to.

16. Introduction to G. Wilson Knight's, *The Wheel of Fire*, p. xiv.

CHAPTER IV

1. Perhaps it is worth remarking that a particular interest of *À la Recherche du Temps Perdu* is Proust's analysis of 'appearance', of how we come to see things as other than they are, because of ignorance, habit, social pressure, or some kind of subjective bias such as desire.

2. There are three excellent essays on this play, by G. Wilson Knight in *The Wheel of Fire*, by D. A. Traversi in *Scrutiny*, VII, 3 (December 1938), and by Henri Fluchère in *Shakespeare*, pp. 211 ff.

3. There is a marked element of stylization in the presentation, as when Cressida is kissed by each of the generals on her arrival in the Greek camp (she is handed around like a puppet). The play is not peculiar in this. Where it is peculiar is in the formal debating of the issues, and in the deliberate reference of certain characters, outside the framework of the play, to their known characteristics in legend.

4. As expressed by Ulysses for example in lines 197-210 of the scene in which the 'order' speech occurs:—

> They tax our policy, and call it cowardice;
> Count wisdom as no member of the war. . . .

5. First, according to Mr K. Deighton, the editor of the Arden edition of the play, by Churton Collins in *Studies in Shakespeare*. To the instances quoted from Churton Collins may be added 'The unity and married calm of states' (I. iii. 150), which seems to echo a passage in *Alcibiades*, I. 126. Whether Shakespeare derived his knowledge directly from a Latin version of Plato or mediately from another source does not concern us here. Mr W. J. Craig (I again draw on the Arden note) pointed out that the maxim, 'the eye that sees round about itself sees not into itself', occurs in Nashe's dedicatory epistle (to the Earl of Southampton) of *The Unfortunate Traveller* (1594). In an article in *The Hudson Review* (I. 3), '*Troilus and Cressida* and Plato', I. A. Richards claims to find the 'strange fellowship' of Plato and Shakespeare throughout the play.

6.   For that will physic the great Myrmidon
> Who broils in loud applause.

(I. iii. 377-8)

7. 'Virtue', it may be noted, does not seek 'remuneration'. It is only the Renaissance 'virtú' that seeks applause.

8. Shortly after the passage just quoted Ulysses touches on the 'mystery' of state:

> There is a mystery, with whom relation
> Durst never meddle, in the soul of state,
> Which hath an operation more divine
> Than breath or pen can give expressure to.

It is one of the play's many ironies that these lines occur when Ulysses is in process of revealing himself as head of the Greek Intelligence Service (the phrase is Dr Richards's):

All the commerce that you have had with Troy
As perfectly is ours as yours, my lord.

(III. iii. 202-7)

The 'state' that Ulysses stands for is soulless.

9. Mr Traversi says, 'Troilus' terminology is indefinite and the expression of his argument, like so much of the discussion in this play, is far more complicated than its content.' Wilson Knight's interpretation of 'will' as instinctive, unconscious passion' ('The suggestion is that the lover sees his own soul reflected in what he loves. He awakes to self-knowledge by seeing') seems to me to fit neither the immediate nor the wider context. Cressida later makes an apt comment on this speech: 'The error of our eye directs our mind. . . . Minds sway'd by eyes are full of turpitude' (v. ii. 106-8).

10. Here, as in the passage last quoted, there is the same sense of grasping at an experience that cannot be articulated 'with distinct breath' (cf. 'lose distinction') and realized.

11. In proceeding directly from *Troilus and Cressida* to *King Lear* I am, I know, taking a large stride. Some may find it too large for any adequate demonstration of a connexion; it covers too much ground, and thereby obscures too many matters that might introduce awkward complications: in short I am over-simplifying. Since the charge on the face of it would not be unreasonable I should like to make here two observations. The first is that the book does not claim to do more than to suggest the main lines of a pattern of development; and clearly there *are* dominant interests that connect one play to another, even though other plays that (so far as we can tell) come between may show a more or less complete redirection of attention. Professor C. J. Sisson's lecture, 'The Mythical Sorrows of Shakespeare' (*Proceedings of the British Academy*, Vol. XX, 1934), is a memorable warning; and the fact that *Twelfth Night* belongs to the same period as *Hamlet* reinforces the remark made above (p. 60) to the effect that even Shakespeare's deepest preoccupations were not obsessions. In the second place, many of the plays written in the years immediatley preceding *King Lear* are in fact closely connected in theme and controlling interest; this is notably the case with those that express Shakespeare's interest, early revealed, in man's subjection to the power of illusion—'the seeming truth which cunning times put on To entrap the wisest'. I should like briefly to indicate the significance of this particular grouping.

The question posed by the undoubted power of illusion branches in two directions, towards the deceiver, and towards the deceived. Shakespeare, like many another writer, was certainly interested in the deceiver, especially the one who does not merely assume a deliberate disguise, like Iago, but is false in subtler ways, like Cressida, or deceives himself as well as others, like Angelo. But in the period under consideration his main interest seems to have centred on the deceived, and a question to which he returns is how men come to make false or distorted judgments about other persons or about the world at large —what it is in their own natures that makes them capable of being deceived. That there is this preoccupation in other plays besides *Troilus* there is no doubt. It is present in *Much Ado*, where the credence given to the slanderer may well be intended to precipitate a judgment on the society represented by Claudio and Don Pedro. (See the essay by James Smith in *Scrutiny*, XIII, 4.) It is present in *All's Well*— that unsatisfactory play, which only makes sense when it is seen as a kind of morality in which Bertram is for long unable to recognize his true good in Helena. Above all, it is present in *Othello*, where attention centres on those elements in Othello's mind and feelings, his attitudes towards himself, that make him so vulnerable to Iago— as F. R. Leavis shows, I think conclusively, in his essay in *The Common Pursuit*.

Now in all these plays the wrong judgments are completely wrong. In *Julius Caesar* and *Timon of Athens* the interest shifts to the distorting intrusion of subjective elements, even when the facts of the case as presented are such as go a long way to justify the hero's view of the world. A large part of the interest of *Julius Caesar* lies in the attempt made by the leading characters, notably by Brutus, to maintain too rigid a distinction between 'public' and 'personal' concerns ('for my part, I know no personal cause to spurn at him, But for the general'), and in the consequent element of unreality in the public action. Of *Timon* I would say here that it seems to me very clear indeed that what is presented for examination is the relation between Timon's 'bounty' and his misanthropy. In other words, the question concerning the validity of Timon's judgment of society is subordinate to the question, How did Timon come to feel like this? how does a man reach such extremes of hatred and rejection? And the conclusion to which the play leads us is that although Timon, in his denunciation of Athens, of mankind, may say some true things, he speaks from an attitude that is itself flawed. Since the purpose of his bounty seems to have been, at least in part, to purchase a flattering picture of himself, the misanthropy that results when the picture is destroyed is in effect a violent expression of self-dislike; and this is true even though the world of the play presents plenty of matter for denunciation. Similar considerations are, I believe, relevant to *Hamlet*. The world with which Hamlet has to deal is indeed evil, and the play shows convincingly the logic of corruption;* but the emotions and attitudes that Hamlet brings to bear when he confronts that world are themselves the subject of a radical questioning.

In all these plays, then, though with varying degrees of intensity of concern, we find we are pondering questions of a kind that are prompted by Blake's dictum, 'As a man is, so he sees'. And it is Shakespeare's increasingly clear perception of the intricate and intimate relations of 'self' and 'world' that points, once more, to *King Lear*, where, it may be remarked, it is inescapably clear that deceiver and deceived meet in one person.

Chapter V

1. Hardy of course comes to mind; and we may turn also to Leopardi's '*La Ginestra*' (1836).

These slopes (of Vesuvius)
Let him come visit who is wont to exalt
With praise our mortal state; here let him judge
With what a loving mind
Nature tends humankind. . . .

Nature recks not, and cares
No more for what befalls
Mankind than for the ant. . . .

(*The Poems of Leopardi*, edited and translated by Geoffrey L. Bickersteth, pp. 341, 351.)

2. 'Even the love of "order" which is thought to be a following of the ways of Nature, is in fact a contradiction of them. All which people are accustomed to deprecate as "disorder" and its consequences is precisely a counterpart of Nature's ways. Anarchy and the Reign of Terror are overmatched in injustice, ruin and death, by a hurricane and a pestilence'—thus Mill.

* See Professor H. D. F. Kitto's closely argued chapter on the play in *Form and Meaning in Drama*.

171

3. *The Works of George Herbert*, edited by F. E. Hutchinson, pp. 116 ff. (I do not understand the half line about the baths.) The same idea is expressed more simply in the poem 'Man'.

> Man is all symmetrie,
> Full of proportion, one limbe to another,
> And all to all the world besides:
> Each part may call the furthest brother:
> For head with foot hath private amitie,
> And both with moons and tides. . . .
>
> For us the windes do blow,
> The earth doth rest, heav'n move, and fountains flow.
> Nothing we see, but means our good,
> As our delight, or as our treasure:
> The whole is, either our cupboard of food,
> Or cabinet of pleasure.

4. *Of the Laws of Ecclesiastical Polity*, Book I, Chap. viii, Sect 1. (Everyman edition, Vol. I, p. 174.)

5. Maurice Castelain, in his valuable edition of Ben Jonson's *Discoveries* (pp. xxii and 68-71) points out that Jonson's prose version of the passage in *The Staple of News* (*Discoveries*, 101) derives from Seneca; he might also have added Boethius (*De Consolatione Philosophiae*, Book II, prose v). In the *De Monarchia*, Book I, chap. xiv, Dante remarks that 'everything superfluous is repugnant to God and nature, and everything repugnant to God and nature is bad (as is self-evident)'—*Dante's Latin Works* (Temple Classics), p. 164.

6. Other causes were of course at work as well. For example, the discovery of new lands, where institutions and forms of behaviour were radically different from those of western Europe, suggested that the 'natural' was only the customary. Montaigne's essay 'Of the Cannibals' is well known.

7. F. T. Perrens, *Les Libertins en France au XVIIᵉ Siècle*, p. 82. *La doctrine curieuse des beaux esprits de ce temps ou pretendus tels* of Fr. Garassus appeared in 1623. In ' "Thou, Nature, art my goddess": Edmund and Renaissance Free Thought' (*J. Q. Adams Memorial Studies*, ed. J. G. McManaway and others), R. C. Bald quotes a similar maxim of the free thinkers as formulated, and controverted, by Father Garassus: 'There is no divinity or sovereign power in the world but Nature, whom we must needs satisfy in everything, refusing to

NOTES

our body and senses nothing that they demand from us in the exercise
of their natural powers and faculties'.

8. There is much more relevant material throughout the play, especially in
Act II, scene iv, from which the last quotation comes.

9. Recent studies have handled with some fulness the changing back-
ground of ideas reflected in *King Lear*. I should like to refer especially
to the following:—Theodore Spencer, *Shakespeare and the Nature of
Man*, Chapters I and II; R. C. Bald, ' "Thou, Nature, art my goddess";
Edmund and Renaissance Free Thought', in *J. Q. Adams Memorial
Studies*, ed. J. G. McManaway and others; H. B. Parkes, 'Nature's
Diverse Laws: the Double Vision of the Elizabethans', *The Sewanee
Review*, LVIII, 3, Summer 1950. An earlier essay on Renaissance
free thought is L. I. Bredvold's 'The Naturalism of Donne in Relation
to Some Renaissance Traditions', *Journal of English and Germanic
Philology*, XXII (1923) pp. 471 ff. Important interpretations of *King
Lear* are made by John F. Danby in *Shakespeare's Doctrine of Nature:
a Study of 'King Lear'*, and by Robert B. Heilman in *This Great
Stage: Image and Structure in 'King Lear'*, and both set the play in
the light of contemporary conceptions of 'Nature'. With whatever
reserves as to detail, or indeed at times as to critical method, I am
conscious of a debt to both these authors which I should like to make
explicit: as also an obvious and continuing debt to G. Wilson Knight,
particularly to his brilliant essay in *The Wheel of Fire*, 'Lear and the
Comedy of the Grotesque'. The pages devoted to Lear's Fool by Miss
Enid Welsford in *The Fool: his Social and Literary History* (pp. 253 ff.)
offer some penetrating comments on the play as a whole.

An essay by W. R. Keast, 'The "New Criticism" and King Lear'
(*Critics and Criticism, Ancient and Modern*, ed. R. S. Crane, pp. 108 ff.),
should be noticed here. Keast criticizes Heilman because his method
'necessitates treating the very premises on which the characterization
and action of the play depend for their intelligibility as if they were
not premises but unsolved problems'. Heilman, he says, suggests that
'such fundamental questions as whether nature is a moral order in the
universe are not determined until the end of the play'; whereas, on
the contrary, 'The reader knows from the outset, and does not have
to wait for the ultimate dissolution of a system of dichotomies to learn,
that the view of nature put forward by Edmund is, in all essential
respects, wrong' (pp. 129-31). In other words, Shakespeare assumes
from the beginning, and expects his audience to assume, a moral order
against which we can judge the characters and evaluate their actions
in specific circumstances.

173

I am not sure that we need accept such rigid alternatives as these: *either* Shakespeare was unable to resolve the problems raised by *King Lear* until he had almost finished writing it (which is indeed unlikely) *or* he stated his action in terms of an unquestioned moral order. Certainly *King Lear* is not a play without moral presuppositions, but although these presuppositions are finally reaffirmed, and thereby deepened and renewed, hostility and blindness towards them are so strongly built into the play's structure that one can only suppose that it took shape as a result of a fundamental questioning.

10. See Theodore Spencer, *Shakespeare and the Nature of Man*, pp. 135-52—pages to which I am considerably indebted.

11. See A. C. Bradley, *Shakespearean Tragedy*, 266-8. Bradley's Lectures on *Lear* in this volume should certainly be read by the student of the play.

12. The nature of Lear's madness is often misunderstood, as when, for example, Dr Leslie Hotson, in an interesting essay, attributes it to his suffering, or 'the stunning blows of his ungrateful daughters' cruelty' (*Shakespeare's Motley*, pp. 99, 101). Even Miss Welsford attributes Lear's madness to the action of his daughters—that is, to something external to himself: 'As Lear looks into Goneril's heart his wits begin to turn'. 'The real horror lies not in the fact that Goneril and Regan can cause the death of their father, but that they can apparently destroy his human integrity' (*The Fool*, pp. 261-2). As both Heilman and Danby have insisted, Regan and Goneril represent aspects of Lear's own personality: it is only in this sense indeed that they can 'destroy his integrity'.

13. As Granville Barker pointed out, Lear *acts* the storm: see his essay on the play in *Prefaces to Shakespeare*, First Series. It is worth noticing with what effective economy, in the last twenty lines or so of Act II, it is prepared for and, from the first, associated with the king's 'high rage'. The first direction for 'storm and tempest' occurs as Lear declares,

> This heart
> Shall break into a hundred thousand flaws
> Or ere I'll weep. O Fool! I shall go mad.

This is followed, as Lear goes off, first by Cornwall's almost casual 'Let us withdraw, 'twill be a storm', then by further references—severely practical on the part of Regan and her husband, with pity for the king on the part of Gloucester—in which the portentous note

NOTES

is unobtrusively deepened. It is whilst Cornwall's last words are still
echoing in our ears

 —Shut up your doors, my lord; 'tis a wild night:
  My Regan counsels well: come out o' the storm—

that Kent enters to the accompaniment of 'Storm still'.

14. The significance of this in relation to the basic design of the play has
been well put by Mr Norman Maclean. 'At the end of this episode
(IV. vi), the world that Lear tells Gloucester he should be able to see
even without eyes is one in which man is levelled to a beast and then
raised to the most fearful of his kind. . . . The beliefs that have become
the protagonist's by Act IV, scene 6, are his antagonists'—Goneril's,
Regan's, and Edmund's—who also hold that sex and self are the sole
laws of life. Lear has indeed "veered around to the opposite"; it is
as if the tortured came to have the same opinion of the rack as the
inquisitors.'—'Episode, Scene, Speech, and Word: the Madness of
Lear', in *Critics and Criticism, Ancient and Modern*, edited by R. S.
Crane, pp. 599-601.

15. This is a truth insisted on by Coleridge throughout his work, as in his
reference to 'what we can only *know* by the act of *becoming*' (*Biographia
Literaria*, ed. Shawcross, Vol. II, p. 216). In *Dream and Reality*:
an Essay in Autobiography, pp. 89 and 184, Berdyaev has some remarks
that are extremely relevant in this connexion.

16. '*Lear* . . . like the hurricane and the whirlpool, absorbing while it
advances'.—Coleridge, *Lectures and Notes on Shakespeare* (Bohn
edition), p. 329.

17. Since *Lear*, dealing as it does with basic elements in the human
situation, is handling not simply 'adult' conflict but the strains of
emotional development as known, however obscurely, to every child,
the following extract from *The Mill on the Floss* (I, x) has its relevance
here. Maggie, in a fit of jealousy, has just pushed Lucy into the mud.

 ' "I shall tell mother, you know, Miss Mag," said Tom, loudly and
emphatically, as soon as Lucy was up and ready to walk away. It
was not Tom's practice to "tell", but here justice clearly demanded
that Maggie should be visited with the utmost punishment: not
that Tom had learned to put his views in that abstract form; he
never mentioned "justice", and had no idea that his desire to punish
might be called by that fine name.'

This is also an appropriate place to refer to Paul Tillich's remarkable
book, *Love, Power and Justice*.

175

18. J. I. M. Stewart, *Character and Motive in Shakespeare*, p. 22. Thus, as Mr Stewart remarks, 'The blinding of Gloucester represents a sort of crystallizing of the element of physical outrage which the imagery holds so massively throughout the play' (p. 23).

19. See G. Wilson Knight, '*Lear* and the Comedy of the Grotesque', *The Wheel of Fire*, pp. 186-8.

20. Dr Johnson has a fine and characteristic comment on Edgar's exhortation, 'Bear free and patient thoughts' (iv. vi. 80)—'To be melancholy is to have the mind *chained down* to one painful idea, there is therefore great propriety in exhorting *Glo'ster* to *free thoughts*, to an emancipation of the soul from grief and despair'.

21. Gloucester's last appearance before his attempted suicide is in iv. i.— a scene that enacts the remarkable statement of Cressida's, 'Blind fear, that seeing reason leads, finds safer footing than blind reason stumbling without fear: to fear the worst oft cures the worst' (*Troilus and Cressida*, iii. ii. 75-7). I have long felt the poignant beauty of the concluding lines surpassed by few single passages in the play.

> GLOUCESTER. There is a cliff, whose high and bending head
> Looks fearfully in the confined deep;
> Bring me but to the very brim of it,
> And I'll repair the misery thou dost bear
> With something rich about me; from that place
> I shall no leading need.
> EDGAR.   Give me thy arm:
> Poor Tom shall lead thee.

I do not think it is a merely personal reaction to find here—in some unanalysable effect of tone and movement—something corresponding to the more marked counter-turn of Cordelia's reappearance.

22. Professor Kenneth Muir, in a note on this line in the Arden edition, quotes W. Perrett—'When Cordelia is away her place as the representative of utter truthfulness is taken by the Fool'.

23. References to Enid Welsford, *The Fool: his Social and Literary History*, are to pp. 253 ff. I am conscious of a very considerable debt to Miss Welsford's promptings.

24. For Kent, Lear is not only the embodiment of 'authority' (i. iv. 32), he is 'thy master, whom thou lov'st' (i. iv. 6), 'Good King' (ii. ii. 160), and 'the old kind King' (iii. i. 28), all of which may in some measure prepare us for Cordelia's almost incredible 'the good man' (iv. iv. 18).

NOTES

25. Richmond Noble (*Shakespeare's Biblical Knowledge*, p. 231) refers to *Wisdom*, vii. 3, and Professor Muir, in the Arden edition, to Montaigne (tr. Florio,) and Holland's *Pliny*. To these may be added St Augustine's, 'We begin our life with tears, and therein predict our future miseries' (*The City of God*, XXI, xiv). It is also worth remarking that in *The City of God*, XXII, xxii, Augustine's description of the overwhelming miseries of this life is not unlike what we are given in the storm scenes of *King Lear*.

26. We should be aware of the unobtrusive and unforced references that give the scene such concreteness and immediacy: thus Cordelia prays,

> Restoration hang
> Thy medicine on my lips, and let this kiss
> Repair those violent harms. . .

and her gaze travels from 'these white flakes' to 'this face' and back to 'this thin helm'. The few simple actions are indicated with a similar economy, as in Lear's 'let's see; I feel this pin prick', in Cordelia's 'No, Sir, you must not kneel', and in Lear's 'Be your tear's wet? Yes, faith'. With this last we may recall how far Lear has travelled since, in one of those revealing phrases of his earlier self, he referred to 'women's weapons, water drops' (II. iv. 279).

27. D. G. James, *The Romantic Comedy*, p. 121. In his later book, *The Dream of Learning*, Mr James clearly brings out the play's affirmative qualities as 'a peculiar labour of knowing'. Mr James's account of Shakespeare's development from *Hamlet* to *King Lear*, and his comparison between the knowledge involved in *King Lear* and the knowledge that Bacon was eager to promote, are alike illuminating.

28. See Paul Tillich, *The Courage to Be*, especially pp. 152-3, 159 ff.

CHAPTER VI

1. See note 9 to Chapter V, above.

2. Leone Vivante, *English Poetry and its Contribution to the Knowledge of a Creative Principle*, p. 18. See also Coleridge, 'On Poesy or Art', *Biographia Literaria*, ed. Shawcross. Vol. II, pp. 257-8.

3. Baudelaire, 'Correspondances'. That Baudelaire goes on from this fine opening to discuss questions of synaesthesia is perhaps unfortunate but irrelevant.

4. Wilson Knight, in his perceptive study of the play, ' "Great Creating Nature" ' (*The Crown of Life*), speaks of it as 'an all-powerful presence,

M 177

at once controller and exemplar'. But even for nature in *The Winter's Tale* 'all-powerful' is not precisely the right adjective.

5. It is of course common for good and evil to be compared respectively to beneficent and harmful or unpleasant aspects of nature,—as we might speak of bounty as a harvest or miserliness as a black frost. But in *Macbeth* analogies for human good are found in the *general* process of nature, whereas evil is defined solely in terms of what is perverse or abnormal in nature, and is constantly described as ''gainst nature' or 'unnatural'. Nature, we are made to feel, is on the side of good and disowns evil. See Wilson Knight's essay on 'Life-Themes in *Macbeth*', in *The Imperial Theme*.

6. It is indeed impossible to make a sharp distinction between harmful 'weeds' and beneficent 'simples'. According to the notes in Professor Muir's Arden edition, fumitory 'was formerly employed in cases of hypochondrism and black jaundice', darnel has narcotic powers, and hemlock is used as a narcotic as well as a poison. Compare Friar Lawrence's soliloquy, in *Romeo and Juliet*, II. iii., on earth's 'baleful weeds and precious-juiced flowers',—

> Many for many virtues excellent,
> None but for some, and yet all different . . .
> For nought so vile that on the earth doth live
> But to the earth some special good doth give;
> Nor aught so good but, strain'd from that fair use,
> Revolts from true birth, stumbling on abuse . . .
> Two such opposed kings encamp them still
> In man as well as herbs, grace and rude will. . . .

This passage is quoted in Edgar C. Knowlton's 'Nature and Shakespeare' (*P.M.L.A.*, LI, 1936, pp. 718 ff.), which sees Shakespeare's conception of Nature in relation to traditional thought, and lists many interesting passages.

7. D. A. Traversi discusses the complex imagery of this passage in his *Approach to Shakespeare* (p. 78), and in his chapter on Shakespeare's last plays in the Pelican *Guide to English Literature, 2, The Age of Shakespeare* (p. 258).

8. It is, I think, in the injunction, 'Spring with my tears', that Shakespeare establishes the close kinship of human nature and the wider nature from which it is born. Taken by itself, of course, the phrase is not particularly remarkable; it is only in its context that it has this subtle force of suggestion. But there seems no end to the subtle

interrelationships of imagery in *King Lear*. Thus one has only to linger on the adjective 'unpublish'd' to see its small but significant part in the counter-movement of the play. Elsewhere the emphasis is on hidden corruption, 'what plighted cunning hides', 'undivulged crimes', and so on. But there are also 'bless'd secrets' and 'unpublish'd virtues'.

9. 'The main element in Jacobean pessimism had been the conviction that evil, including its destructive potentialities, was natural. . . . But the dominant theme of *Macbeth* , a theme reiterated by all the leading characters and in most of the major scenes, is that evil is unnatural. Nature, however inscrutable, is basically beneficent, and such a crime as Macbeth's is not in accordance with nature but contrary to it.'—H. B. Parkes, 'Nature's Diverse Laws: the Double Vision of the Elizabethans' (*The Sewanee Review*, LVIII, 3, Summer, 1950). This is a valuable and stimulating essay. The second quotation is taken from Leone Vivante, *English Poetry and its Contribution to the Knowledge of a Creative Principle*, p. 29.

10. In Sonnet CXXIV there is an interesting contrast between self-seeking and disinterested love. The first is assimilated to the merely natural world,

> As subject to Time's love or to Time's hate,
> Weeds among weeds, or flowers with flowers gather'd;

the second is described as 'builded far from accident'—that is, it is a human achievement. But in the human order what is 'built' (we may say, deliberately sought and willingly fostered) has life in it,—

> And ruin'd love, when it is *built* anew,
> *Grows* fairer than at first, more strong, far greater.
>
> (Sonnet CXIX)

11. Too full, that is, 'to catch the nearest way'. Lady Macbeth invariably uses euphemisms for murder—'must be provided for', 'this night's great business', 'our great quell'.

12. Hobbes, *Leviathan* (Everyman edition), I, 13, p. 65. 'The Passions that encline men to Peace', says Hobbes, 'are Fear of Death; Desire of such things as are necessary to commodious living; and a Hope by their Industry to obtain them' (p. 66)—which is true, but only part of the truth.

13. See 'The Milk of Concord: an Essay on Life Themes in *Macbeth*', in *The Imperial Theme*, especially pp. 140-1, 144-5, 148-51. In contrast, Macbeth projects onto Nature his own malice; for example at III. ii. 13-15—

M*   179

> We have scorch'd the snake, not kill'd it;
> She'll close, and be herself; whilst our poor malice
> Remains in danger of her former tooth.

We do not need to ask ourselves what the snake is that will 'close'. Macbeth is dimly aware of a hostile world with which he is committed to an unending struggle.

14. *The Imperial Theme*, p. 142. F. R. Leavis, in 'How to Teach Reading' (*Education and the University*, pp. 122-4) gives a characteristically sure and sensitive account of the imaginative effect of the first ten lines of this scene.

15. Parallels between *Macbeth* and *Lucrece* are noted by Professor Kenneth Muir in Appendix C of his Arden edition of the play. Of 'defect' in the lines quoted above, where a slight immaturity of style cannot conceal the maturity of the thought, C. Knox Pooler, in a note in the Arden edition, says, 'Probably . . . "the absence of what is really present" rather than "something lacking to our possessions" '.

16. This is symbolized by the banquet scene (III. iv) where the formal ceremony of the opening ('You know your own degrees, sit down: at first And last, the hearty welcome') contrasts with the 'admir'd disorder' of the close. Macbeth's inner chaos—'confusion', now, having 'made its masterpiece'—is similarly reflected later in the unco-ordinated violence of his 'royal preparation' for the battle, on which the Doctor dryly comments (v. iii. 57-8). 'Sin is an act of violence in itself,' says Benjamin Whichcote; 'the sinner doth force himself, and stirs up strife within himself'.—F. J. Powicke, *The Cambridge Platonists*, pp. 75-6.

17. Savage nature is not insisted on as it is in *King Lear*, but the repeated references to birds of prey and to those members of the animal kingdom for which men tend to feel some instinctive dread or repugnance—shark, tiger, wolf, etc.—do not allow us to forget that aspect of the play's background.

18. So too 'boundless intemperance' is 'a tyranny' (IV. iii. 66-7).

19. Two articles by L. A. Cormican on 'Medieval Idiom in Shakespeare' (*Scrutiny*, XVII, 3 and 4) contain many pregnant reflections on the relation of moral to psychological insights in this play and in Shakespeare generally, and on the relation of both to the prevailing tradition.

20. Walter Clyde Curry, *Shakespeare's Philosophical Patterns*, p. 105.

21. Middleton Murry, in a chapter of his *Shakespeare* significantly called 'The Time has been', catches the sinister significance of the dubious

phrase, but I cannot properly understand the conclusion to which he proceeds.

22. T. S. Eliot, *The Rock*.

23. 'No evil passion pursued to the end,' says Berdyaev, 'has any positive content. All evil consumes itself. Its nothingness is laid bare by its own inner course of development. Evil is the sphere of phantasy (an idea admirably developed by St Athanasius the Great). Evil is evil not because it is forbidden but because it is non-being.'—*Freedom and the Spirit*, p. 183. The same idea is expressed in the *Revelations of Divine Love*, by Julian of Norwich: see especially Chapters XI ('Sin is no deed'), XXVII, and LXIII. The traditional doctrine of the essentially negative quality of evil, with especial reference to *Macbeth*, is admirably described by Walter Clyde Curry in *Shakespeare's Philosophical Patterns*.

CHAPTER VII

1. See 'The Transcendental Humanism of *Antony and Cleopatra*' in *The Imperial Theme*.

2. *Prefaces to Shakespeare, Second Series*, p. 146.

3. Shakespeare, Granville-Barker rightly says, 'is never the vindictive moralist, scourging a man with his sins, blind to all else about him' (*Op. cit.*, p. 196), and the play certainly emphasizes Antony's admirable qualities, especially his ability to make friends with the men he commands and his generosity. But it is in this very respect also that Shakespeare shows himself so far from 'blind'. When Antony reproaches 'the hearts . . . to whom I gave their wishes', we are compelled to ask, What had he given? The answer of course is, gifts ranging from kingdoms to mule-loads of treasure—visible and tangible symbols of worldly power. He has 'play'd' as he pleased 'with half the bulk o' the world . . . making and marring fortunes' (III. xi. 64-5); 'realms and islands were As plates dropp'd from his pocket' (v. ii. 91-2); and at his call 'kings would start forth', 'like boys unto a muss' (III. xiii. 91). If all this—which forms the background of his bounty—is felt as discandying it is, surely, not just because Antony is defeated, but because it is of the very nature of the wealth that he deals in to betray an exclusive trust. It is certainly vain and arrogant pomp that is insisted on in the account of the distribution of the kingdoms in Act III, scene vi:

I' the market place, on a tribunal silver'd,
Cleopatra and himself in chairs of gold
Were publicly enthroned . . .
. . . she
In the habiliments of the goddess Isis
That day appear'd . . .

The resounding catalogue of proper names (ll. 14-16, 68-76) is to the same effect. I do not think it matters that the description is made by the unsympathetic Caesar; Shakespeare need not have dwelt on it at such length, and the fact that he does so suggests that he was deliberately following Plutarch's lead: 'it was too arrogant and insolent a part, and done . . . in derision and contempt of the Romans' (*Shakespeare's Plutarch*, ed. C. F. Tucker Brooke, Vol. ii, p. 86).

4. A view of the play in some ways similar to this is expressed by Professor John F. Danby in *Poets on Fortune's Hill: Studies in Sidney, Shakespeare, Beaumont and Fletcher*, Chap. v. '*Antony and Cleopatra:* a Shakespearean Adjustment'. An excellent description of the imaginative effect of the passage from the play next quoted in my text is given by Mr L. G. Salingar in his essay on 'The Elizabethan Literary Renaissance', in the Pelican *Guide to English Literature, 2, The Age of Shakespeare*, pp. 106-9.

5. Martin Buber, *I and Thou* (translated by Ronald Gregor Smith), p. 48.

6. Wilson Knight, in his essay on *Coriolanus* in *The Imperial Theme*, shows how city life is constantly present to us in imagery and allusion.

7. The Tribunes are not admirable, but it is a Tribune who gives the just and necessary comment on Coriolanus's character:

You speak o' the people
As if you were a god to punish, not
A man of their infirmity.

(iii. i. 79-81)

John Palmer, in a valuable essay in *Shakespeare's Political Characters*, points out that it is the 'conservative' Coriolanus who is only too anxious to abrogate 'custom' when it doesn't suit his wishes.

8. See D. A. Traversi's essay on the play in *Scrutiny*, Vol. VI. No. 2.

9. The phrase was coined by Ian D. Suttie in *The Origins of Love and Hate*, Chap. VI. The taboo on tenderness he saw as a defensive reaction—a sour-grapes attitude—to bad psychological weaning:

those who embrace the taboo and hold up ' "toughness", aggressiveness, hardness, etc, as prime virtues' are really carrying on into adult life a form of infantile protest; they can't afford to be anything but 'tough', not having reached an adequately grounded maturity that would allow them to admit gentleness and tolerance into companionship with their strength. See also D. W. Harding, *The Impulse to Dominate*, Chap. XIV.

10 In an article on '*Coriolanus*, Aristotle and Bacon' (*Review of English Studies*, New Series, I. 2. 1950) F. N. Lees aptly applies to the play Aristotle's remark, 'He that is incapable of living in a society is a god or a beast'.

11. Wyndham Lewis, *The Lion and the Fox*, pp. 202-3 and Part VII. Chapter II.

12. *Jerusalem*, IV. 83.

CONCLUSION

1. For Coleridge on Shakespeare as philosopher see *Biographia Literaria*, ed. Shawcross, Vol. II, p. 19; *Lectures on Shakespeare* (Bohn edition), p. 242 and *passim*. The book by Virgil K. Whitaker is *Shakespeare's Use of Learning: an Enquiry into the Growth of his Mind and Art*, and my quotation is from p. 277. The quotation from Leone Vivante will be found in his book, *English Poetry and its Contribution to the Knowledge of a Creative Principle*, p. 3: on the distinction between 'poetic thought' and 'the thought of the poet' see p. 122, and T. S. Eliot's Preface, pp. ix-x. Agamemnon's speech is from *Troilus and Cressida*, I. iii. 3 ff. 'The possible other case' is borrowed from Henry James, who says of irony that it 'implies and projects the possible other case, the case rich and edifying, where the actuality is pretentious and vain' —Preface to *The Lesson of the Master*, p. x.